THE UNIVERSAL PROVIDER

By RICHARD S. LAMBERT

★

THE RAILWAY KING

THE PRINCE OF PICKPOCKETS

THE INNOCENCE OF EDMUND GALLEY

WHEN JUSTICE FALTERED

MEMOIRS OF THE UNEMPLOYED

WILLIAM WHITELEY, THE UNIVERSAL PROVIDER

Fr. From *Fortunes Made in Business*

THE UNIVERSAL PROVIDER

A STUDY OF WILLIAM WHITELEY AND THE RISE OF THE LONDON DEPARTMENT STORE

by

RICHARD S. LAMBERT

ILLUSTRATED

" I'll get you a hedgehog at once," he said; " they're sure to have some at Whiteley."

ALDOUS HUXLEY

ACKNOWLEDGMENT

MY sincere thanks are due to Mr H. Gordon Selfridge and to the Directors of William Whiteley, Limited, for granting me access to the archives of the business, which date back in some cases to the year 1867. These archives, including particulars of sales, leases, and accounts, provide a factual backbone to the narrative of William Whiteley's achievement in building up London's first department store. Some of the archives are water-stained, and all those that cover the earlier years are difficult to decipher and interpret correctly. I therefore owe also a debt of gratitude to Mr A. H. Warton, the Secretary of William Whiteley, Limited, for his invaluable help in sorting out and explaining the various records which I required. I am likewise deeply indebted to Mr A. E. Cowper, a Director of William Whiteley, Limited, for giving me information and advice on the business aspects of shopkeeping. Mr Cowper also enabled me to establish essential personal contacts for the furtherance of my researches, and facilitated the loan to me of the firm's copy of the great catalogue of 1885, as well as of an early bill of 1864, which I reproduce among the illustrations to this book. I desire in addition to thank Mr P. A. Best, formerly Managing Director of Shoolbred's, for giving me an outline of the development of that business, at one time the best-known rival to Whiteley's. Finally, I wish to acknowledge the courtesy of a number of London shops in supplying me, at my request, with particulars of their origin and early history.

R. S. L.

CONTENTS

ILLUSTRATIONS

CHAPTER I

Dream and Reality

ABOVE the elms on the southern edge of Hyde Park, browned by the August sun, rose the shining walls of Paxton's giant glass house that held the Great Exhibition of 1851. The dream of a nation of shopkeepers had come true, a fairy-like palace of crystal, rising tier upon tier in a grassy oasis in the midst of a desert of bricks and soot—the largest and dirtiest city upon earth. The palace was pleasantly flanked by lawns, and approached by broad gravelly ways, along which horses could amble and carriages crunch. From outside it looked grander and greater than any building most of its visitors had ever seen—1848 feet long, 408 feet wide, and 100 feet high, gay with the flags that waved from its pinnacles, and bright with the colours, light blue, orange, and scarlet, that adorned its iron framework. Inside were avenues, galleries, and vaults of glass, down the length of which stretched endless vistas of colour and form—the treasure-trove of the world, 19,000 exhibits gathered and laid out on stands and counters for the delectation of man and the increase of trade. Here were the raw products of nature, vegetable, chemical, and mineral. There were the tools and machines, little and big, devised by man to transform nature's materials. And there, too, were the finished manufactures, foodstuffs, textiles, hardware, furniture, buildings, pottery—every kind of object of luxury or necessity. The whole place resembled a gigantic shop whose wares had been contributed by the peoples of every continent to show how they could, if trade were properly organized, serve one another. But the trading remained a dream, for you could not buy the treasures displayed in the palace; you could only look at them. It was an exhibition, not a shop.

The Exhibition had been open since May, and as the entrance-fee had been steadily reduced from a pound to five shillings, half a crown, and one shilling, it was patronized by enormous crowds of sightseers of all classes—43,000 a day on the average, coming from all parts of the kingdom and from abroad. The spirit that animated these sightseers, nourished as they strolled through the glass alleys by buns and mineral waters, was that of a gigantic picnic. Confusion and demoralization had been feared, but in fact order and good humour everywhere prevailed. Employers sent their workmen, farmers their labourers, clergy their parishioners, and schools their children to see the fairy palace, by train and steamer, coach and cart, on horseback or on foot. One day during the height of this holiday rush there was to be seen moving through the Exhibition a short, stocky young man with ruddy cheeks and a queer, rather repressed smile upon his lips. He came obviously, as his accent and dialect showed, from South Yorkshire; yet he seemed less rough than the usual Yorkshire 'tyke'—in fact, his manner smacked of Southern politeness as he edged his way from stand to stand, closely observing what was displayed on each. He was in his twentieth year, and his name was William Whiteley. He was one of four sons borne by Elizabeth, daughter of Thomas Rowland, to her husband, William Whiteley, who followed the pursuit of corn-factor at Agbrigg, near Leeds. Young William was born on September 29, 1831; and in the following June the family removed from Agbrigg to Purston, a village six miles from Wakefield and two and a half from Pontefract. Here the boy was brought up, obtaining his schooling first at the neighbouring village of Featherstone, next at Ackworth, and lastly in the town of Pontefract. The district was rich in coal, but mining had not yet developed so far as to spoil its rural character. From the first young William led an open-air life, and was interested (through his father's trade) in farming. The claims of school cannot have been very serious, since by the age of ten he was already experienced enough on horseback to hunt regularly with the Badsworth Hounds, then allowed to be the best, strongest, and fastest pack in the land. His father was of sufficient means and standing to provide his son with a mount and to secure him a place in the Hunt. Wrote William Whiteley sixty years later:

> I used to ride a little snow-white pony under thirteen hands, and with a wonderfully hard mouth, so that it was quite impossible for me to hold her; all that I could do was to stick on, and away she used to go with my small self sticking to her like a limpet. Nothing could stop her, five-barred gates, stone dykes, high hedges, wide streams—she either went over or through them, and I never once knew her refuse.[1]

The Badsworth Hunt brought the boy into distinguished company. It included Lord Hawke and his brother, Stanhope; Sir Charles Greaves, who weighed

[1] "In the Days of My Youth," by William Whiteley, in *Mainly About People*, November 8, 1902.

twenty stone; and above all John Gully, "prize-fighter, horse-racer, legislator, and colliery proprietor." Gully was about fifty when William Whiteley came to know him, a tallish man with piercing eyes under bushy brows and with a tight-lipped, sarcastic mouth. It was many years since he had stood in the ring, but he could tell boys entrancing tales of how he had fought the Lancashire giant Bob Gregson in 1807 and knocked him out in the twenty-eighth round. Still more, he could initiate any youngster interested in horses into the whole art and craft of racing; for Gully had enjoyed a long and lurid career as a trainer, backer, and owner of racehorses, and had won both the Derby and the St Leger in the year after young Whiteley's birth. Then, his colliery speculations having made him a rich man, he had chosen to enter Parliament as member for Pontefract. Though, as Greville spitefully remarked in his *Diary*, "there appear no reasons why the suffrages of the blackguards of Pontefract should place him in different social relations towards us than those in which we mutually stood before," in fact Gully became accepted by Society, his sons obtained commissions in the Services, and he himself was presented at Court. After a few years, however, he tired of politics, and retired to Ackworth Court, his residence, to resume the life of country gentleman, hunter, and racehorse-owner and -backer.

This was the time when Whiteley came under the notice of Gully. Whiteley was "the baby of the Hunt."

> I remember the first time I was on I was fifth in at the kill. They were going to give me the brush, but a lady came up and it was given to her, and I had to be content

with the promise of it another time—a promise, I may say, faithfully fulfilled. The members of the Hunt were very proud of me, and very kind, because they thought me a real good sportsman, as whenever the meet was anywhere near my home I was always there, no matter what the weather might be. And when, after a long run, we called at the nearest gentleman's house and had the usual crust of bread, piece of cheese, and horn of home-brewed ale, they always took care that I was not overlooked and had my full share, Mr Gully in particular paying me special attention.

When he was fourteen and a half years old William left school finally, and spent two years at home, working on his uncle's farm near by.

During this time [he tells us] I had a thorough insight into Yorkshire farming, the knowledge then gained being of great service when later on I started my own farm as part of my business. . . . I worked well, and sometimes played well. I was very fond of horses and riding, also shooting, and I think I can safely say that by the time I was sixteen there were not many better riders or better shots in the 'horsy' and 'gunny' county of Yorkshire than myself.

An anecdote of Gully illustrates the point:

I recollect being at work in one of our fields one day when he rode up in the next field, where two ponies were running loose, and speaking to me over the hedge asked whether I thought I could catch Dick, one of the ponies. I replied that I did not know, and he said he thought I could not, but that if I could I was to ride him home and keep him. I at once got a piece of rope and set off to try my luck, and after a very hard struggle I caught Dick, rode him home in triumph, and kept him.

This must have been about the year 1846, when

Gully won both the Derby and the Oaks. What a hero he would seem to the young farmer!

During the two years while he was living at home Whiteley obtained glimpses of the wider world by making tours on horseback in company with a celebrated bonesetter and veterinary surgeon, Dr Taylor, who apparently travelled about the country attending to the needs of man and beast. On these tours young Whiteley had many strange experiences; but at length it became necessary for him to think of settling down and beginning to earn his own living. No opportunity presented itself for him to become a farmer, but for a while it seemed as though he might be able to turn to account his talent for riding. He thought, indeed, of becoming a jockey, no doubt with the hope of encouragement and patronage from Gully, who could ' pull strings ' for him at Newmarket. But the prospect never materialized, and a much more humdrum profession had to be sought. In June 1848 his parents apprenticed him, now in his seventeenth year, to Messrs Harnew and Glover, the largest drapery in the neighbouring town of Wakefield. The term was for seven years, during which he was given, in his own words, " a severe drilling in the arts and mysteries of trade."

Life in a country drapery at this time offered few excitements. In almost all such establishments the shop depended entirely for custom on its own particular kind of ' connexion '—family, political, or religious, as they were classified.

> If it was a seaport town one draper would perhaps cultivate more especially what may be termed the outfitting branches, such as goods chiefly intended for men's wear, as

shirts, hosiery, and sometimes ready-made clothes and hats —even a few double-barrelled guns might be found, which have been known to sell well with officers and others going abroad. While another draper, perhaps, in the same town would lay himself more open to the country trade, and keep goods more particularly suited for country customers; and these would even keep a few such incongruous articles as smock-frocks and gaiters. Then each was supported again by their fellow religious denominationalists. The Dissenter would be the one to serve the Nonconformist part of the population, while the Churchman would be backed up by the members of the Establishment, who would buy nothing at the other shop unless they were compelled. Personal character went a much longer way than in the present age. The proprietor was looked upon to gossip with his customers and take notice of their little ones.

No doubt Messrs Harnew and Glover's connexion was among the Church people and those of the highest social standing in Wakefield. Their apprentice took his work seriously, and applied himself in his leisure time to Bible-class work on Sundays, falling evidently at this stage of his life under Evangelical influences.

Although he was learning his trade at the biggest business of the kind within his reach, William Whiteley can hardly have been satisfied with the prospect of remaining all his life in or near Wakefield. Once, indeed, Wakefield had been the main seat of the Yorkshire woollen trade, but this had since migrated to Bradford, Leeds, and other places. Now "in the side-streets of Wakefield, where once busy cranes were engaged in hauling up bags of wool all day long, or letting them down into wagons, the grass grows along the edges of the streets, and the cranes hang idle against the walls." It was three years before young William found a chance to look out for any better prospects; but at last he obtained from his employers in the summer of 1851 a holiday—the first since his indentures were signed. He employed it in coming to London to do what so many thousands from all parts of the kingdom were doing—see the Great Exhibition.

We can easily imagine what specially attracted his attention as he wandered through the Crystal Palace. To a young man in his position the sections displaying machinery and manufactures must have been more interesting than the section displaying raw materials. He would not linger long beside the manufacturing machines and tools, or the civil engineering, architecture, and building contrivances—not even the intriguing plan of a scheme to remove all smoke from open house-fires. Nor would the naval architecture, military engineering, and guns mean much to him, except for the fine exhibit of small arms for hunting purposes. But, like every one else, he would surely admire the carriage section, one of the most elegant displays in the Exhibition, which incidentally included new types of fire-engines and pumps driven by steam, with which Whiteley was to become only too familiar at a later stage of his career. His farm training would no doubt cause him to examine the agricultural and horticultural machinery, which included types of steam-ploughs, threshing-machines, and drills, as well as grass-cutters, patent garden watering-engines, and model beehives of curious shapes in the likeness of villas and cottages. Then his eye would be caught by the musical, surgical, and horological instruments—especially the last, for Whiteley loved clocks, and liked to have them keep

THE GREAT EXHIBITION OF 1851 IN HYDE PARK

From a print by George Baxter

By permission of Mr W. T. Spencer

accurate time and all strike together. In this department were the first-fruits of the new art of photography, daguerreotypes and talbotypes, plain and coloured; also curiosities such as Gilbert's patent tooth-extractor and Count Dunin's mechanical figure, which "admits of being expanded from the size of the *Apollo Belvedere* to that of a colossal statue," Newton's planetarium, various specimens of the recently invented electric telegraph, Gall's triangular alphabet for the blind, Nasmyth's map of the moon, and Badcock's photographic specimens of vaccine culture. The musical instruments comprised a fine selection of pianos, including Erard's Elizabethan New Patent Grand Oblique pianoforte, which was built like a set of sixteenth-century carved choir-stalls.

However, it was the third section of the Exhibition—manufactures—which held exhibits of professional interest to a young draper. Pride of place was taken by cottons, followed by woollens, and then silks and velvets—all the exhibits being shown under glass to preserve them from dust and contamination. Over the entrance to the Western Nave, where the silks were found, was a beautiful trophy composed of rich tissues, brocades, damasks, and other furnishing silks, all crowned by a silken banner. Silk was used above all for the manufacture of ribbons—a category of drapery in which Whiteley took a special interest. Here Coventry had displayed its finest products, showing the results of substituting steam-power for hand-weaving. The ribbons from Coventry were distinguished by being ornamented with a pearl edging, and sometimes being clouded in the dyeing.

After the silks came the linens and damasks, with

specimens of material made from the new fibre, jute, which had been recently introduced from the East Indies. Then came the leather and saddlery goods, including skins, furs, and feathers. Here were ostrich plumes and ornamental *toupées*, side by side with Wellington boots with revolving heels and ladies' boots with cork soles. The dyed and printed fabrics would have much to interest the aspiring shopkeeper—chintzes, tablecloths, turkey red handkerchiefs, etc. So would the collection of tapestry, carpets, lace, and embroidery, which included Faudel and Phillips' richly carved State Bed, ornamented with embroidery and fancy needlework. More important for his purpose, however, was the South Transept Gallery, given up to articles of clothing. Here were to be seen hats, bonnets, hose, gloves, corsets, slippers, and all manner of finery for men, women, and children—a gigantic drapery establishment, in fact, all under one glass roof. Then in the North Gallery Sheffield and Birmingham displayed their cutlery and hardware, which included a quantity of metal furniture as well as many ingenious appliances for domestic use. It is not likely that Whiteley would linger long looking at the jewellery exhibit in the South Central Gallery; but he would be more interested in the glass exhibit in the Central North Gallery, where, for instance, Chance Brothers, of Birmingham, were showing large sheets of patent plate-glass, which was coming into fashion for use in shop-windows. There was plenty of variety of bad design to be seen in the china and porcelain exhibit and in the furniture exhibit, both of which gave free play to the Victorian passion for rococo ornamentation. Here was a maze of enormous carved sideboards, huge mirrors decorated with gilt scrolls, pretentious consoles, frilly candlesticks, knobby and spiky armchairs, sofas, and settees. Finally, there were quantities of small wares, and an exhibit of manufactures for building and decoration.

It is easy to imagine the effect of this profusion and variety of exhibit upon the young draper's apprentice as he wandered through the glass galleries and gazed at the contents of the glass cases. Nothing was lacking except the opportunity to handle, carry away, and use the goods displayed; and Whiteley, who was being trained to be a shopkeeper, must naturally have formulated in his mind the image of a vast emporium—a sort of Crystal Palace run on business lines. He could even perhaps picture himself the owner of this emporium—gathering together all these goods from the ends of the earth, displaying them behind great glass windows and dispensing them across spacious counters to multitudes like the crowds that thronged the Crystal Palace—sightseers rather than customers. Whiteley was benevolent and ambitious, and this dream bid fair to satisfy both sides of his nature.

But what a vast gap remained to be bridged between this dream and the reality of shops as they were in 1851! If Whiteley, as was likely after his visit to the Great Exhibition, determined that his future fortunes lay in London, it seems probable that he must have spent the rest of his little holiday in wandering through the streets and noting the principal shopping centres where he would be most likely to secure employment once his apprenticeship had been served.

The shops of London at the time when Whiteley first saw them were passing through a transitional stage corresponding to the vast changes which were taking place in industry. During the Middle Ages there had been more booths and stalls than shops. Then gradually the itinerant huckster had found it worth his while to localize his trade, live above his stall, and build up a 'connexion' of regular customers. Following the traditional practice of markets and bazaars, those who sold the same commodities grouped themselves in the same streets and localities. At first all shops, like the booths from which they sprung, had open fronts and exposed their wares direct before the consumer. But by the eighteenth century open fronts had everywhere, save in the poorest parts, given way to glass windows, small, divided into square panes, and protected at night by heavy wooden shutters. The older type of windows were flat, the more recent bow-shaped. The interior of the shop was dark and cramped, the floor uncarpeted, and the window display primitive. A roll or two of cloth perhaps, with a few men's hats wrapped carefully in paper in the background, would be considered by a draper as providing adequate attraction for his customers. No one but a fool put out in his window more stock than he could help, lest it should become soiled. As a matter of fact, the shopkeeper of the eighteenth century preferred to rely upon his elaborate signboard, of wood or metal, hung out over the roadway from his projecting upper story. This signboard would be sufficient for his regular customers —the 'connexion' upon which he mainly relied for his turnover. The shopkeeper usually lived over his shop with his wife and children, one or two assistants, and the same number of apprentices—a family establishment. The idea of employing a big staff was unknown. In 1800 the largest shop in London, a haberdasher's, employed only sixteen assistants. Nor had any thought of subdividing departments, combining several types of supply under one roof, or joining shop to shop, entered the head of a single tradesman. In short, from the end of the Middle Ages to the beginning of the nineteenth century the London shopkeeper, like his provincial *confrère,* visualized his function rather as that of serving regular customers who sought him out than as that of going forth in search of new clients or attracting into his shop the casual passer-by.

From the end of the Napoleonic Wars, however, a change began to be noticeable. The City Companies, which had hitherto closely supervised the London tradesmen, were in the last stages of decay. Machinery and steam-power had made their way into the textile industries, revolutionizing prices and output and multiplying the variety of goods available. Cheap cotton was coming over from America and displacing the traditional woollen materials used for making dresses. Gas had been introduced for lighting purposes, and was beginning to be used for the illumination of streets and shop-fronts. Then in the eighteen-thirties railways were built, and omnibuses plied their way from one end of town to the other. Shopkeepers found it necessary to watch, attract, and even follow their customers. A residential migration took place in London. Slowly the City began to empty, and while the proletariat occupied (as they always had done) the ' liberties ' to the east and north, rich men commenced to separate their places of business from their homes, which they transferred to the West End. This " West End " was always receding and creating new suburbs that in their turn provided opportunities for new shops. So the tide of shopkeeping flowed in two opposite directions. One part settled in Whitechapel and Aldgate, and sold cheap, flashy goods to the poor; the other part gathered first around St Paul's Cathedral, gradually flowed down Ludgate Hill, crossed the Fleet river into Holborn and the Strand, and eventually reached high-water mark in Oxford Street, Bond Street, and the newly constructed Regent Street. Here were (and are) the luxury shops of London.

As shopkeepers moved westward their manner of doing business necessarily altered under the stimulus of the intense competition to which they found themselves subjected. They were forced to seek out customers instead of waiting for them. At once a change took place in the size and appearance of premises. A shop on Ludgate Hill was the first to take in the first floor and carry its windows soaring up to a double height. This daring innovation was made possible only by the invention of plate-glass, which—though architectural purists condemned it because " it serves only to produce the effect of a vast gap or vacuum, and take away all appearance of support to the upper part of the house "—at once made window display an art worth cultivating. The traditional shapely gilt letters announcing the name of the shopkeeper and his trade were now taken down and replaced by others of wood or glass, considered more likely by their oddity of shape or richness of ornamentation to catch the eye of the passer-by. Such letters were either made very thick and squat or very thin and lofty, or thick where they should have been thin and *vice versa*, or set out in perspective as if standing one behind another like a file of soldiers, or set vertically up the front of the house, or—in at least one instance—placed upside down. A similar catchpenny motive inspired the dressing of windows. Any device, however undignified, was resorted to to arrest the attention of passers-by. Slips printed with the words "Look Here!" "Stop!" "Tariff," "Income Tax," or "Given Away" were pasted on the inside of the glass. And in times of slack trade it was usual to exploit the discovered weakness of the customer for buying damaged goods at an imagined reduction. To read the notices blazoned in the shop-windows one might almost imagine that man was made to fatten on the misfortunes of his fellow-man. Here the eye might catch the inscription "Dreadful Conflagration," there "Awful Inundation," "Manufacturing Distress," "Ruinous Sacrifice," "Bankruptcy." Such written horrors were intended to make the customer believe that these misfortunes enabled the shopkeeper to sell countless bales of goods at less than the cost of the bare materials. It was long before the joke became a stale one or was worn to death by constant usage. Occasionally a shopkeeper more inventive than his fellows would improve upon even these pretended disasters. A small but real fire might be made the occasion of a vast 'sale' of goods imported and specially singed for the purpose. Alternatively, stock supposed to be salvaged from a wrecked vessel might be eked out with drapery goods that had been laboriously dipped in salt and water by the assistants before the shop doors opened.

Apart from these dodges there were other drawbacks to shopping in the West End. The time-honoured system of fixing prices by bargaining between seller and purchaser had only just begun to go out of fashion. The method of having one price, and one price only, for each article in a shop was being adopted in the larger establishments, where the increase in the size of the staff made bargaining less attractive to the shop-owner, since he could no longer personally control its operation. Shops where no bargaining was done were now snobbishly proud of their new standard of honesty. Should a customer try the old-fashioned method,

> the assistant thinks at first that you have misunderstood him. But when he realizes what you are driving at he stiffens visibly like a man of honour to whom one has made a shady proposal. He gives you to understand politely but plainly that his prices, being equitable, cannot be reduced. His resolute bearing is so unmistakable that only a fool would insist.[1]

It was, in fact, the customer rather than the shopkeeper who bewailed the old custom. So ingrained had become the habit of first selecting an article and then chaffering over its price that when the new plan came into operation many customers seemed to have lost half their interest in shopping. Women, especially the more elderly, prided themselves upon the tact and management which they displayed in getting goods cheaply, and resented the loss of their opportunities. And the fixed-price system brought its own problems. Shops where the fixed-price system prevailed usually displayed a conspicuous notice saying "No Abatement" in their window. But this did not always imply

1 *A Frenchman Sees the English in the Fifties,* adapted from the French of François Wey by Valerie Pirie (1935).

that prices were easy to identify. For the device had been soon discovered of ticketing a commodity equivocally, so as to deceive the casual eye. Thus, for example, two guineas, by a dexterous smallness of the pound sign, might be made to look remarkably like twenty-two shillings.

Drapers and other tradesmen were just beginning to study the art of arranging goods attractively behind plate-glass. Since stands were not made in those days, the enterprising salesman had to make use of boxes or rolls of cloth. Upon these he spread out rows of goods—say, open shawls, one behind another, commencing at a low altitude and gradually filling the window into the back. It was already known that to fill a window with a large number of a single type of commodity or colour was a good way to attract custom; yet it was not usual to make much display of ready-made articles of drapery. Prints, stuffs, and shawls—the heavy goods, as they were called—occupied most of the window space. In this respect the drapers lagged behind other tradesmen—the hatters, for instance, in whose windows you might see a pair of scales to indicate that a certain hat only weighed a certain number of ounces, or a glass globe full of water with a hat swimming on it, to show that it had been waterproofed—all at 4*s.* 9*d.*! Or again the bootmakers, whose varied stock was labelled with the names of contemporary celebrities, such as Wellington, Blücher, Clarence, or Albert.

The attractions and importance of window-dressing had been greatly increased by the discovery of gas, which introduced the possibility of shopping by night until ten or eleven, or even midnight. Gas and glass went well together. The enterprising shopkeeper found that he could cast a meretricious sheen over his goods by displaying them behind plate-glass lit by rows of dazzling flares suspended above or in front of his windows. Inside the shop an equally grand effect could be produced by imitating the Ludgate Hill pioneer who first adopted the plan of clothing his walls and ceiling with looking-glass, and causing these to reflect the light from rich cut-glass chandeliers. Thus decorated, the draper's shop achieved a brilliance only surpassed by the gin-palace. No wonder the habits of the shopping public altered, and a demand was created for late closing which was responsible for a sad deterioration of the working conditions of shop assistants.

As the poet Southey put it in his *Letters to Espriella*:

> If I were to pass the remainder of my life in London I think the shops would always contrive to amuse me. Something extraordinary or beautiful is for ever to be seen in them. In one window you see the most exquisite lamps of alabaster, to shed a pearly light in the bedchamber, or formed of cut-glass, to glitter like diamonds in the drawing-room; in another a convex mirror reflects the whole picture of the street with all its moving swarms, or you start from your own face, magnified to the proportions of a giant. Here a painted piece of beef swings in a roaster to exhibit the machine that turns it; while another window displays every sort of artificial fly for the angler. And thus there is a perpetual exhibition of whatever is curious in nature or art, exquisite in workmanship, or singular in costume; and the display is perpetually varying, as the ingenuity of trade and absurdities of fashion are ever producing something new.

All these exterior improvements made obsolete the former outstanding feature of the shop-front—the signboard. It vanished, to reappear in new forms—the poster, the handbill, and the peripatetic placard. By the eighteen-forties the "external paperhanger," clad in fustian jacket with immense pockets, armed with paste-box suspended by a strap, placard pouch, and a set of thin telescopic rods tipped with a cross-staff and capable of reaching the loftiest elevation at which

PERAMBULATING HAT
From Knight's *London,* vol. v (1843)

posting bills is legible, was a familiar sight in London streets. So too was the more genteel bill-distributor, whose task it was to insinuate advertisements gracefully and irresistibly into the hands of passers-by; also the sandwichmen, trailing in procession, and by mere multiplicity of numbers achieving notoriety through their interference with the traffic. To the peripatetic placard succeeded the vehicular, and Regent Street was enlivened by the sight of a spirited horse dashing along in front of a gig shaped like a gigantic hat to advertise Perring's light hats, or a Thespian cart adorned with a structure of Gothic arches and pinnacles, in whose niches stood headless busts clad in the latest fashions, the whole slowly revolving by means of some internal clockwork as the vehicle passed by.

The changes in methods of advertising goods and attracting custom were paralleled by similar changes in the interior economy of the West End shop—or 'emporium' as it preferred to call itself. The old-fashioned draper's shop had few departments, and needed but few assistants to serve in them. His goods fell into two classes, 'heavy' and 'fancy,' the former consisting of prints, stuffs, and shawls, the latter of lace, ribbons, gloves, and so forth. It was from the 'heavy' class that the draper derived his chief revenue, for in those days he sold scarcely any made-up goods, since women invariably made their own dresses or bought the materials from the draper to have them made up by the milliner or the dressmaker. As dresses were of great length and fullness, eight or nine yards of stuff was the usual complement purchased. The assistant's chief skill was therefore displayed in the handling and display of large rolls of material. Silks, for instance, of which the most luxurious dresses were made, were kept rolled on blocks; and in order to display a roll to the best advantage the assistant was required to manipulate it with considerable skill. Seizing the end of the piece of silk with one hand, he must dexterously twist it round two or three times, curl the end underneath, and pop the fabric down under the customer's eye loosely puffed up in a heap, so as to show off the lightness or shade of the material. The first made-up goods to be sold by drapers were women's cloaks—long, straight garments with little pretension to style, that reached down nearly to the feet and were accompanied with capes—both made generally of coloured merino wools, dark brown, dark drab, or green.

The fancy departments in those days were undeveloped, and yielded but a small part of a draper's returns. A few standard articles were always kept in stock, such as the coloured twilled squares used for ladies' and children's necks and known as Barcelona handkerchiefs, plain silk fabrics worn by boys, called romals, men's black silk neckerchiefs and black satin squares, scarves, stocks and ties, and 'stiffeners' for collars of various heights. But none of these articles were displayed on counters or in windows. They were kept in square mahogany boxes, whose front let down at pressure upon a spring, to enable the customer to make his choice. Made-up stocks with bows attached, scarves of figured satin or cashmere, shawl borders (sold by the yard), lace (for caps), and thread-edgings were sold in quantities. Gloves and hosiery were also included in the 'fancy' class of goods, but customers were not encouraged to finger, examine, or try on goods. In the fifties François Wey reported the greatest difficulty when he was shopping in inducing an assistant to show him more than two fingers of a pair of gloves which he was contemplating buying. The ribbon department usually contained rich brocaded gauze ribbons a quarter of a yard wide, which were popular for bonnets, and plain lute-strings nearly as thick as belt ribbons. Ribbons were in demand for watch-strings and for fastening shoes and sandals; yet so small was the turnover that it was not uncommon for a roll of fancy ribbon to be kept in stock for from two to five years. Lastly there was haberdashery of a clumsy sort—the most unpopular because the most laborious department in the shop. There thread had to be separated from the bulk in the pound packet and made up into skeins by hand, the operation being performed by sticking a yard-measure upright into two leathern loops attached to one part of the counter for the purpose, a device which in the hands of a tyro often produced a hopeless tangle. Similarly skeins of silk were laboriously made up by hand in bundles rolled in sheets of paper, leaving the tops—a brilliant, variegated mass of colour—exposed for customers to draw out their choice of shade.

In running his shop the draper usually employed at least two buyers, one a 'drapery buyer' in charge of the heavy goods, the other a 'fancy buyer' in charge of the smaller and lighter articles. Upon the enterprise, taste, and thriftiness of these buyers depended largely the success of the business. The buyers were therefore set in authority over the assistants and apprentices who made up the rest of the staff. The latter were expected not merely to serve behind the counter, but also to undertake the rough work which, as the organization of shops became more elaborate, came later to be performed by regular porters. It was the task of the lads, for instance, to take down the heavy shutters soon after six each morning, and clean the brass name-plates of the firm, the outside of the windows, and the lamp-glasses or gas-globes which illuminated them. Apprentices did not expect much in the way of comfortable quarters for themselves. Shops in London were usually cramped for space, and as most of the staff lived in on the premises it was not uncommon for the lads to have to sleep in pairs on truckle-beds kept under the counter. The adult assistants, of course, had a separate room, where they slept, washed, and 'dressed' themselves for service after breakfast.

The great drawback to a shop assistant's life was the length of his working day. Formerly the apprentices and trade assistants of London had been noted for their vigorous and healthy frames, independent bearing, and fondness for athletic exercises; but the gradual substitution of a class of paid assistants for the more domestic relationship of the past inflicted untold hardships on these employees. Twelve hours a day, including two for meals and relaxation, was by prescription and custom all that a master was entitled to in return for a day's wages. The working day usually began at eight in the morning, and, according to Defoe in his *Complete British Tradesman*, nine in the evening was the latest hour for closing. But already by 1800 this time was being exceeded, and as shops became larger and artificial lighting more effective the twelve hours were lengthened to thirteen, then to fourteen, and so on—until by the middle of the century the only limit to shop labour was the power of endurance of the assistant: in fact, the custom fast changed into one decreeing the maximum of exertion as the minimum of service. Fifteen, sixteen, and on Saturday even longer hours became common—and often the entire Sunday had to be sacrificed as well. Hours of work were lengthening in industry as well as in trade; and this forced the working man, who was usually paid his wages on Saturday night, to defer his weekly shopping until Sunday morning, which thus became one of the best times for trade.

The miserable conditions of London shopmen are well illustrated in contemporary literature by Samuel

Warren's portrait of Tittlebat Titmouse, the hero of his novel *Ten Thousand a Year*, a best-seller of the early eighteen-forties. The young man soliloquizes in his garret:

> What a life mine is, to be sure. Here am I, in my eight-and-twentieth year, and for four long years have been one of the shopmen at Tag-rag and Company's, slaving from half-past seven in the morning till nine at night, and all for a salary of thirty-five pounds a year and my board. And Mr Tag-rag—eugh! What a beast!—is always telling me how high he has raised my salary! Thirty-five pounds a year is all I have for lodging and appearing like a gentleman.

Titmouse, vain, inconstant, and addle-pated, was employed in an Oxford Street drapery by Tag-rag—"a great tyrant in his little way. A compound of ignorance, selfishness, and conceit," who "knew nothing on earth except the price of his goods and how to make the most of his business." Bully and toady—this was how employer and employed appeared to Society readers, as presented by the pen of the fashionable novelist.

A shop assistant might be expected to receive in London from twenty-five to forty pounds a year in wages as well as his board. In many shops he could supplement this to a considerable extent by earning premium money, or 'tinge' as it was called—commissions on the sale of goods. Where the premium system was in force it led to various abuses due to excessive zeal. There were assistants who prided themselves on selling goods to customers at prices higher than those marked on the tickets. Others would not let customers go once they had entered the shop. There was in employment a trick known as 'the swap,' which consisted of taking an unsatisfied customer to another part of the shop and showing him some of the goods which he had already rejected, pretending that they were something new or special, and so inducing him to buy them. Customers were often bullied into buying goods they did not want. They were 'reasoned' with in the most forcible manner, and it was proved to them by demonstration that that which was sought to be forced on them was the very thing they wanted. A veteran draper confesses:

> Many a half-frightened girl have I seen go out of the shop, her purchase in her hands, the tears welling up in her eyes, shaking her head and saying, "I am sure I shall never like it"—some shawl or dress having been forced upon her contrary to her taste or judgment.[1]

By premiums it was possible for the ordinary assistant to add from twelve to fifteen shillings a week to his wage, or, in the case of assistants selling specially fashionable articles such as shawls, from twenty to twenty-five. On the other hand, there were shops where no premiums at all were paid. Here it was not uncommon for the assistants to display an apathy which many customers could hardly distinguish from rudeness. François Wey described as amazing the detached attitude of such salesmen. "In London," he wrote in 1856, "shopkeepers do not extol their wares; they seem quite indifferent whether you make or do not make a purchase." When he had bought his pair of gloves

> the cashier took my money with the attitude of a man receiving a subscription for some charitable purpose, and

[1] *Reminiscences of an Old Draper* (1876), p. 8.

my parcel was handed to me by the shopman with a benevolent expression as though he were making me a small gift. Sometimes, even, they seem so averse to parting with their goods that you feel you are depriving them of cherished possessions.

The handling of money in a shop was still managed in primitive fashion. Each assistant received payment from the customer he served, went himself to the till, and took out the required change from its appropriate divisions, gold, silver, or copper. Obviously there was room for mistakes in such a system, particularly in the bigger shops, where it began to be superseded by the employment of boys as messengers between the shopmen and the cashier. A few of the largest establishments were now taking between one and two hundred pounds a day and employing as many as fifty hands in all, including a new type of assistant, known as a 'shopwalker,' whose duty it was to direct customers to the right counter. A great fuss was always made over 'carriage customers,' who, being supposed to cast lustre on the shop they patronized, were received with special politeness by the draper, his shopwalker, and the assistants. All shopmen with any ambition paid great attention to the neatness and fit of their own dress. It was possible for a handsome young assistant with superior manners to become a favourite with ladies of distinction among the shop's customers; then they would signify a preference to be served by him when they came into the shop; and so he might begin to form a 'connexion'—a step on the way towards setting up in business on his own. On Sundays, when the young shop assistant was often turned out of his lodging, he would promenade in Kensington Gardens,

" CARRIAGE CUSTOMERS " IN REGENT STREET DURING THE LONDON SEASON

From *The Illustrated London News,* March 31, 1849

dressed like Tittlebat Titmouse in a frilled calico shirt with linen wristbands, white trousers, flowered damson-coloured silk waistcoat, blue surtout with embossed silk buttons and velvet collar, sky-coloured kid gloves, top-hat, and black, gilt-headed cane—in which attire he would pass anywhere for a gentleman. Nor was it unknown for the same fashionable customer who preferred to be served by her favourite assistant in the shop to 'notice' him with a nod when her carriage passed him on the sidewalk in Hyde Park. But all this finery and pretentiousness was kept for Sundays only. On week-days after shop hours the young men used to spend their evenings in a public-house, where they would smoke together, sing naval, sentimental, and bawdy songs, and often reel home in the small hours of the morning the worse for liquor. Naturally the master discouraged such proceedings; fines were imposed on those who slipped out from the shop to drink, and these were deducted from premiums at the end of the week.

No clear distinction had yet emerged between retail and wholesale shopkeeping. A large draper or milliner, for instance, might become known for the excellence of certain of his departments or lines of goods. This would attract hawkers or other persons anxious to start in business on their own account, who would purchase goods from him in bulk at wholesale rates. In due course, to avoid misunderstandings, different parts of the shop would be set aside for the different classes of customers, wholesale and retail. And so the same draper might carry on simultaneously both branches of the trade, extending the range of the former as the more enterprising of his shopmen left him in due course to set up small shops of their own. Perhaps, as he grew old, this draper would abandon retail trading altogether, and specialize in wholesale trading; or, as happened frequently in London, the tide of shopping moved away westward and left his retail business unprofitable.

This was the condition of affairs just beginning to arise among the City shops at the time of the Great Exhibition.

CHAPTER II

Bankruptcy Avenue

NEARLY four years passed before the young apprentice could realize his ambition of visiting London again. His indentures expired in 1855, when he became qualified to practise as journeyman the trade of draper's assistant. On the very day after their expiry Whiteley left Wakefield, to seek his fortune in the city of his dreams. Paxton's palace had by this time left Hyde Park, but not London; for only a short while before Whiteley's return it received its rebirth by transmigration to Sydenham Hill, where it was reopened with pomp and ceremony by Queen Victoria on June 10, 1854, as a centre for popular culture and amusement. The dream to which it had given birth—a great emporium of the world's trade—remained locked away in Whiteley's mind. Towards its realization he possessed, when he reached London in 1855, a paltry ten pounds, apart from his unshakable determination to bring it about. But first he must gain experience. For the next eight years he set himself systematically to master every detail of the London drapery trade. Already he had made up his mind to start in business on his own without any partner as soon as he could satisfy himself that the way was clear. He was blessed with great self-reliance, had a clear knowledge of his own powers, knew what he lacked, and set himself to obtain it. He concentrated on work alone, and had no other hobby.

But first he must choose where to settle in order to

gain the experience he wanted. London now possessed several distinct shopping centres, some old-fashioned and on the downward grade, others progressive and subject to fierce competition. We can imagine Whiteley, before choosing his employer, setting forth on a tour of inspection. Beginning from the east end of the City, he would traverse first several wide thoroughfares, Shoreditch, Whitechapel, and Aldgate, where the shops were gaudy and pretentious in appearance, but stocked mainly with cheap and trashy goods suited to the poorest class of consumers. There were two big drapery establishments in Shoreditch: John Hopkins, who occupied three houses with his large linen, woollen, and silk warehouses, and Rotherham's, who concentrated mainly on the wholesale trade. From Aldgate he might traverse the financial quarters of the City without coming on any important shops, though as he crossed Gracechurch Street he might catch sight of a fine old business, dating from 1750—that of Spink and Son, who, as well as being goldsmiths and jewellers, sold sporting guns. Beyond the Bank he would pass down first Poultry and then Cheapside, which consisted of "well-built, lofty houses, the lower parts of which are warehouses and well-supplied retail shops." In the latter were situated two large cottonwear houses and an establishment of silk dealers, besides the chemist's shop of G. Butler, which claimed to have been founded in 1616. On the north side of Cheapside, occupying the whole space between King Street and Ironmonger Lane, stood the dignified offices of the Atlas Assurance Company.

If Whiteley, pausing here, were to turn northward and stroll along Aldermanbury past the establishment of Bradbury and Greatorex, he would eventually find himself close to London Wall, at Fore Street, where stood one of the best-known drapery establishments in town, brought thither by Joseph Todd in 1799 from its first home in Eastcheap, and later built up mainly by the efforts of James Morrison, a Wiltshireman of Scots parentage, who married Todd's daughter and was admitted to partnership in proverbial fashion. The firm then became known as Todd and Morrison until the admission of a fresh partner, an Irishman named John Dillon, at Todd's death, when it became known as Morrison and Dillon. The frequent changes of name led to the firm's being better known in the City, both in the nineteenth century and now, as the Fore Street Warehouse. The Fore Street Warehouse combined both retail and wholesale forms of trade, but as the former tended to decay in the City it turned over more and more to the latter.

At the west end of Cheapside the tourist would turn left into St Paul's Churchyard, then surrounded by shops that for half a century had been regarded as the last word in elegance and fashion. The north side of the Churchyard was given over chiefly to retail, the south to wholesale businesses. Probably the largest establishment, occupying four houses on a corner site north-west of the cathedral, was that of George Hitchcock and Sons, silk-mercers, linendrapers, haberdashers, and carpet-manufacturers. This tall, handsome shop, fronted with Ionic columns, possessed the largest plate-glass windows in town, and since it employed no horizontal sash-bars—only vertical ones made of brass—it contrived to present (to the wonder of shoppers) "an uninterrupted mass of glass from the ceiling to the ground." It was also the first shop to adopt exterior artificial lighting for its window display. Inside Hitchcock's exhibited rich silks from Spitalfields and Lyons, velvets from Genoa, shawls from China, France, and Paisley, ribbons from Paris and Coventry, delicate laces from Valenciennes, Honiton, and Buckinghamshire, and carpets from Kidderminster, Brussels, and the more costly looms of Axminster. "Capricious indeed must be the fancy of the fair visitor who, whatever may be the nature of her wants from these vast and varied stores, cannot gratify her every wish."

Next door to Hitchcock's stood another drapery, Hall and Allen's, of Waterloo House; and on the south side of the Churchyard was a big china, glass, and earthenware depot belonging to Green and Sons. From St Paul's Churchyard the wanderer might either turn back into Cheapside and go along Newgate Street towards Holborn or else leave the Churchyard by its west end and descend Ludgate Street and Ludgate Hill. The latter disputed with St Paul's Churchyard the claim to possess the finest shops in London. At Nos. 9 and 10 Ludgate Street stood Everington's, renowned for its rich India shawls, many of which, it was rumoured, had been smuggled in without paying customs dues by the wives of Indian Army officers and officials of John Company. These shawls made Everington's windows seem brighter than those of other drapers. Then at Nos. 15 and 16, next to Creed Lane, was Willey's, another drapery; and at the foot of Ludgate Hill, where Fleet Street began, Robert Waithman, the famous Alderman of the City, had built up a business similar to Everington's but rather less specialized, dealing in damasks, muslins, and shawls.

Waithman's career as a member of Parliament well illustrates the contempt in which shopkeepers were held by the aristocracy in the first half of the nineteenth century; for when he attempted to address the House his speeches were almost invariably drowned by the deliberate coughs, hiccups, and snuffles of his snobbish fellow-members.

From Waithman's shop up Fleet Street to Temple Bar and the Strand there were few outstanding shops, but near Charing Cross in Cockspur Street stood another substantial drapery store, that of Howell and James. If Whiteley had preferred following the northern route leading westward from St Paul's he would first have descended Newgate Street, and then gone up Snow Hill, passing through a distillery quarter, flanked, not inappropriately, by a group of undertakers, whose shops dotted Farringdon Street. As he entered Holborn by way of Snow Hill and Charterhouse Street he would pass on his right Hatton Garden, which accommodated, besides diamond merchants' offices, a fashionable carpet repository and the famous Rowland's Macassar Oil and Kalydor Warehouse, "patronized by Her Majesty and the Royal Family." This much-advertised hair-oil manufactory played into the hands of the drapery and furnishing business by creating the demand for antimacassars! Holborn was, of course, lined with shops, but trade did not particularly flourish here, and was already tending to move farther westward. Bending to the south along Broad Street, the wanderer would now enter Bloomsbury, then a fashionable residential quarter, and so reach Oxford Street along New Oxford Street, laid out in 1847 through the disreputable rookery of St Giles'.

Before entering it, however, Whiteley might have walked northward up Tottenham Court Road to a graceful building fronted with two-storied Ionic columns and comprising three houses, Nos. 154, 155, and 156. Here was situated the business of Shoolbred, Cooke and Son, linen- and woollen-drapers, silk-mercers, and carpet warehousemen, which advertised itself as " without exception the largest of any in their department in London, with a larger stock and greater choice of every description of drapery and furnishing goods than at any other warehouse in the kingdom." The fortunes of this firm, founded in 1820, had been built up by the energy and enterprise of James Shoolbred, who, dying in 1845, had passed on the business in a flourishing condition to his son, James. Shoolbred's set out to cater for the aristocratic inhabitants of Bloomsbury, and prided itself on supplying only goods of the highest and most expensive quality. It was beginning to find among its customers a demand that it should extend its activities into fields wider than drapery. In Tottenham Court Road already at this time furniture shops were beginning to multiply. Close to Shoolbred's, for instance, stood the growing business of Maple's, founded in 1842, while farther down the road at No. 203 the widow Fanny Heal and her son carried on the feather-bed and mattress manufactory started in 1810 at Rathbone Place by John Harris Heal. They had recently purchased the " Millers' Stables " at No. 196, and were now living in a quiet, pleasant house set in a flower garden and trees well back from the main road.

Back in Oxford Street the first large shop to be encountered as one walked westward was Jackson's, formerly Jackson and Graham, upholsterers and cabinet-makers, at Nos. 37 and 38 on the north side. Established now twenty years, it promised the purchaser that he might "here rely on meeting with articles executed with the greatest taste by skilled workmen, and at the most moderate prices, the proprietors being enabled to ensure these advantages from the magnitude of their operations and its attendant advantages." In the carpet manufactory were exhibited fabrics in the style of Gobelin, while the shop also stocked "a rich and varied collection of bronzes and porcelain, embracing some of the most magnificent articles ever introduced into England." A few doors farther on stood another large shop, Commerce House, occupied by Williams and Sowerby, general linen merchants. Besides comprising Nos. 61 and 62 Oxford Street, this fronted on to Nos. 3 and 4 Wells Street. It claimed to be "one of the most remarkable commercial establishments in this or any other country, no less conspicuous as an ornament to the street than celebrated as a resort for the most fashionable." Here were conducted both a wholesale and a retail business. Pushing on past a flourishing haberdashery shop at No. 103, founded in 1833 by Peter Robinson but not yet expanded to its later size, the traveller would come at No. 111 to Williams and Hatton, another big drapery that specialized in shawls, lace, gloves, fine cambrics and linens, and, above all, silk stockings. "Here the aristocracy and gentry are supplied with all the magnificent and tasteful fabrics (in constant succession) for ladies' dress that art can invent and wealth can procure." Finally, farther down Oxford Street the enterprising drapery of Marshall and Snelgrove, founded

REGENT STREET

From *Twice Round the Clock*, by George Augustus Sala

by James Marshall just before Queen Victoria's accession in 1837, had outgrown its original premises at 11 Vere Street, and had taken a frontage in Oxford Street at the angle between Oxford Street and Vere Street. Here the firm had put in 1851 a new building known as the Royal British Warehouse. Not far from Marshall and Snelgrove's, also out of Oxford Street, but in Wigmore Street (No. 44 and adjacent houses), was another growing drapery business, that of Debenham and Pooley, whose origin dated back as far as 1778.

These, then, were the biggest shops in and about Oxford Street. But Regent Street on the whole held even more brilliant and fashionable establishments. At the northernmost extremity, where the Queen's Hall and St George's Hall now stand, was the London Carriage Repository of Marks and Son. Then at the end of Regent Street near Oxford Circus stood (at Nos. 247–249) the Mourning Warehouse of W. Checkall Jay and Son, founded about the same time as Marshall and Snelgrove's. This was not a cheerful-looking place from the outside.

> The sober hue of its decorations, contrasting in a striking manner with the gay and cheerful aspect of those by which it is surrounded, must at once attract the attention of the most casual observer, and induce him to desire to know something of the nature of its business. . . . Here may be had every variety of mourning attire, from that which heartfelt affection dictates for the loss of a fond parent or dearly beloved relative to the slight token which friendship or fashion demand, in the newest and most approved material and style, and at a few hours' notice.

As well as mourning attire Jay's sold all kinds of millinery.

But the biggest and best-known shop in Regent Street was at its lower end, Swan and Edgar's, silk-mercers, linen-drapers, and hosiers, at 47, 48, and 49 the Quadrant. This business had been founded in 1812 by George Swan on a site occupied to-day by the Criterion Restaurant, and migrated into Regent Street about

SHOP IN REGENT STREET
From Knight's *London*, vol. v

1818, when the street was first built. Most of the original shops in Regent Street failed to pay their way, but Swan's, under the control of Swan's partner and successor, William Edgar, not only survived but became familiar to Londoners through appearing in the prints of the time (by Cruikshank and others). Its prominent position at the corner between Piccadilly and Regent Street gave it a special advantage, and the shop's style of architecture was praised as

presenting the appearance of sufficient solidity and strength,

> and not looking as if likely to be crushed by the upper part of the house; for, although spacious, the windows are of lofty upright proportions and arched, besides which there is some substance in the piers to which the columns supporting those arches are attached, and where the angle of the building is curved off that space presents a broad solid pier, enriched with panelling.[1]

The artist Doyle and his journalist coadjutor, Percival Leigh, have between them immortalized the interior of a typical Regent Street shop (probably Swan and Edgar's) at the time of the Great Exhibition. In Doyle's *Prospect of a Fashyonable Haberdasher hys Shope* we see the rich 'carriage customer,' trailing her two prim daughters in her wake, sail down the centre of the shop past the posturing shopwalker to join "some sixty or eighty ladies sitting before the counters, examining the wares, busy as blue-bottle flies at a sugarmash." The shop is heated by an oil-stove in the centre of the floor, and lit by pendent gas-lamps in the windows and globes round the counters. Behind the latter stand

> the shopmen and assistants, showing off the goods, and themselves also, with mighty dainty airs, every one of them almost Narcissus his Image. But I fear me they owe their pale, delicate looks and languid ways in part to the want of sufficient air and exercise; which is a sad consideration.[2]

Their methods are urgent and solicitous. No sooner is one purchase completed than, says the salesman "in his soft, condoling voice, 'What is the next article?' as though taking for granted that another was wanted—which was too true." A collar needs four pairs of lace

[1] Knight's *London*, vol. v.

[2] *Manners and Customs of ye Englysshe*, by Richard Doyle and Percival Leigh (1849).

cuffs to match it at twelve shillings. " And now, Mem (meaning Madam)," says the young fellow with a simper, " allow me to show you a love of a robe, a Barège, double *glacé*, brocaded in the flouncings, and

MANNERS·AND·CVSTOMS·OF·Ye·ENGLYSHE·IN·1849 No 2

A PROSPECT·OF·A·FASHYONABLE·HABERDASHER hys·SHOPE.

From *Manners and Customs of ye Englysshe*

reduced to twenty-one shillings and sixpence from forty-five shillings." This bargain snapped up, a blue and scarlet shawl is offered, at two guineas, and then " a superior assortment of ribbons." A dozen pairs of silk stockings at twenty-four shillings round off the orgy of buying, and the martyred customers are " bowed out of the shop by the smirking shopwalker, rubbing his hands and grinning, as obsequious as could be."

New and Old Bond Street struck the sightseer as

> wide and noble, lined by stately mansions of the nobility and gentry, or the scarcely less handsome shops, where wealth, elegance, and fashion is exhibited on every side, and where the individual may not only walk in safety, but have his eye delighted by the grandeur of every surrounding scene.

Here were situated most of the establishments entitled to carry the Royal Arms, as a sign that they were patronized by the Queen and the Royal Family.

Piccadilly was not renowned for the size and importance of its shops, though Fortnum and Mason's had been established there since the time of Queen Anne. At the bottom of Coventry Street (No. 16), facing the Haymarket, stood the London Cloth Establishment of W. P. and E. Dudden, claiming to be "*Par excellence* the Waistcoating Establishment of the Metropolis." In King Street, Borough, Southwark, Thomas Lilley was energetically carrying on the manufacture and retail distribution of footwear at the business he had founded in 1835, but had not yet opened a shop in the West End. At Commerce House, Knightsbridge, a smallish drapery business founded about 1820 by a Mr Harvey was taking advantage of a growing suburban trade; and in another suburb farther north, at 53 Lisson Grove, Paddington, Spencer, Turner, and Boldero's were carrying on the drapery shop started under the name of Spencer and Hall about 1840.

In addition to these shops there were certain retail establishments of a distinctive character resembling general stores, but run on the principle of a market or bazaar. They consisted of a large central hall with or without galleries and upper floors, housing stalls or

THE PANTHEON BAZAAR
From *Twice Round the Clock*, by George Augustus Sala

counters rented from the proprietor of the premises. Typical of this was the Soho Bazaar, occuping several houses in the north-west corner of Soho Square, and bringing together stalls at which millinery, lace, gloves, jewellery, and other articles of decoration were sold. The stall-renters, who paid two or three shillings a day each, were bound by a common set of stringent rules imposed by the proprietor of the bazaar.

> A plain and modest style of dress on the part of the young females who serve at the stalls is invariably insisted on, a matron being at hand to superintend the whole; every stall must have its wares displayed by a particular hour in the morning, under penalty of a fine from the renter; the rent is paid day by day, and if the renter be ill she has to pay for the services of a substitute—the substitute being such an one as is approved by the principals of the establishment.[1]

The Soho Bazaar was patronized not merely by the poor; in the height of the London season the long array of carriages drawn up outside its doors proved the extent to which it was visited and used by the well-to-do. Another 'shop' of the same kind, but more showy and pretentious, was the Pantheon Bazaar in Oxford Street. This was entered by a porch and vestibule adorned with statues, whence a staircase led up to a room occupied as a picture gallery, where pictures were sold on commission. The main part of the building, which was surrounded by a gallery, was filled with counters loaded with trinkets.

> On one counter are articles of millinery; on another lace; on a third gloves and hosiery; on others, cutlery, jewellery, toys, children's dresses, children's books, sheets of

[1] Knight's *London.*

> music, albums and pocket-books, porcelain ornaments, cut-glass ornaments, alabaster figures, artificial flowers, feathers, and a host of other things, principally of a light and ornamental character. . . . On one side of the toy bazaar is an aviary supplied with birds for sale in cages; and adjacent to it is a conservatory where plants are displayed in neat array.

In Belgrave Square was another bazaar called the Pantechnicon. Here carriages were the principal class of articles sold, from dress carriages to light gigs, each vehicle bearing a ticket with the price marked on it.

> Another department is for the sale of furniture and consists of several long rooms or galleries filled with pianofortes, tables, chairs, sideboards, chests of drawers, bedsteads, carpets, and all the varied range of household furniture.

There was also a wine department and a toy mart. In Baker Street was a horse bazaar, where carriages, harness, furniture, stoves, and ironmongery were also sold. And Gray's Inn Road had the North London Repository, once the scene of Robert Owen's "Labour Exchange," but since the failure of that experiment converted into a bazaar for furniture and carriages. These bazaars, which evidently supplied the kind of need which is met in the twentieth century by such establishments as Woolworth's, were the nearest approach to department stores that existed when Whiteley came to London. Yet they lacked the essential principle upon which he had founded his own ambition; they were not co-ordinated and directed by a single mind, but were merely casual aggregations of small traders, each operating independently. Whiteley had little to learn from them in the development of his own scheme. It was not here that he chose to seek the experience he needed. Nor did he attach himself to one of the growing drapers in the fashionable West End of London. He preferred to begin among the old-established firms in the City and work his way through shopkeeping practice along traditional lines.

His intention was to pass systematically from one situation to another, always seeking to enter the employment of some firm where he could pick up information and experience in a department which he had not yet mastered. His first position was with R. Willey and Co., whose shop was at Nos. 15 and 16 Ludgate Street. Here he stayed fifteen months, serving behind the counter. Then he decided he knew enough about retailing, and would do well to gain acquaintance with the wholesale side of drapery. One fine morning, accordingly, Whiteley left Willey's, and next day took a situation at the Fore Street Warehouse, which then traded as Morrison and Dillon. It was an outstanding firm, known all over the country, and Whiteley could hardly have made a better choice for his purpose. He remained at the Fore Street Warehouse for the next five years, save for a short break of three months in the middle. This was occasioned by what he called " a very tempting offer " which he had from his old firm, Harnew and Glover's, to return to Wakefield and take the place of a retiring partner. Whiteley hesitated, agreed to go on trial, but soon found that he could never settle down in the Provinces after London; so at the end of the three months he went back to Fore Street, where his old employers were only too pleased to take him again.

It was Whiteley's habit to measure himself against

the various persons whom he came across in the way of business; and whenever he found a man who knew more about any particular branch than he did he would attach himself to that individual until he had learned all that the other could teach him. He now found an opportunity to specialize in one particular department of drapery—ribbons. Two employees of the firm of Leaf and Sons, of Old Change, were about to leave and set up in partnership for themselves. These two were Graham, the foreign-ribbon buyer, and Green, the English-ribbon buyer. The former was a friend of Whiteley's, and was anxious to persuade him to work for the new firm. Whiteley agreed, but apparently the business, launched in 1861, did not prosper; perhaps the unexpected death of the Prince Consort in December adversely affected the ribbon trade. Anyhow, before they had completed a twelvemonth Messrs Graham and Green sold their business to another firm in St Paul's Churchyard and retired from the scene. Whiteley remained with them till their shop was closed, and came away with the advantage of having gained what he wanted—a specialized knowledge of ribbons, particularly of the imported article.

He had now equipped himself for the venture which he had been long planning—to open his own shop. For the past ten years he had lived frugally, neither smoking nor drinking, but saving what he could to accumulate a small capital. Throughout the period he had received a comparatively good salary, which he supplemented by commissions on sales—for he was always an excellent salesman. In this way he put by nearly £700, which seemed enough for his purpose. Moreover, the times appeared propitious for the launching of his ambition, inasmuch as the idea of a department store was already being put into operation on the other side of the Atlantic by A. T. Stewart, the fame of whose palace of white marble with its 2000 employees had spread far beyond New York. But Stewart limited his activities to 'dry' goods only—manufactured articles—whereas Whiteley planned eventually to include 'wet' goods—*i.e.*, perishable articles or provisions. But Whiteley was not the man to take a risk without first investigating the chances of success. He carefully examined the state of the market for foreign ribbons, in which he intended to specialize, and came to the conclusion that prices were too high for him to buy at a profit for the time being. The American Civil War was in full swing; there was a shortage of cotton, and much unemployment and distress in Lancashire. Accordingly, with wise self-restraint he decided to postpone launching his own business for a year, and meantime to take a temporary post with another large wholesale drapery firm in the City, Messrs Bradbury, Greatorex, and Beall, of Aldermanbury. He did not mean, however, merely to mark time; he employed his leisure in active search for the best locality for his future shop.

London was expanding fast in the early sixties, and the numbers of flourishing shops in the main centres of the City and the West End suggested that new enterprise had best turn its attention to catering for the suburbs. But the trade manuals of the time were full of warnings against the suburbs. Thus the *Handy Book of Shopkeeping* declared:

> There is a tendency among small capitalists to rush into new neighbourhoods, thinking to secure the connexion

> when it does come, low rents being a great attraction, forgetting the grave proverb, "While the grass grows the steed starves." We have rarely found that the very early suburban shop succeeds. The few inhabitants prefer to supply themselves from established shops, and the local shopkeeper is only asked to supply wants that accidentally happen. . . . It seems therefore desirable for the small capitalist rather to run the risk of a more expensive rent in a well-peopled district than to resort to places of slow and uncertain demand. . . . The suburban shopkeeper should confine himself to supplying the *necessities* of life. To make a living in the suburbs he must make a 25 per cent. profit on his turnover.

Whiteley, however, *was* thinking of the suburbs. There were two districts which seemed to him to offer possibilities of success. One was Upper Street, Islington, where, however, competition was already very fierce. The other was Westbourne Grove, in Bayswater. Down to 1837 Westbourne Grove was a real 'grove' just outside the entrance to the village of Paddington—a lane flanked on each side with tall trees and banks of wild flowers, with a fine view across the fields to Hampstead Church. The Grove ended at the Royal Oak, where the lane petered out into a track called the Bishop's Path. But in 1837 this rural solitude was rudely interrupted by the construction of the Great Western Railway and the opening of Paddington Station. Then Bishop's Path became Bishop's Road, and small houses were built along both it and the Grove. Their occupiers, however, were mainly humble folk, such as market-gardeners and laundresses. As late as 1852 Westbourne Grove, although it had lost its trees, remained a quiet street, lined with detached cottages, each fronted by its own garden. At the end nearest Paddington was a large, open nursery-garden, which in summer was gay with dahlias, geraniums, and other bedding plants. At the other end was a brickfield where the present Archer Street runs, and between the brickfield and the Grove was an open space where small boys were wont to congregate and fight out their quarrels.

During the ten years before Whiteley saw it, however, Westbourne Grove had undergone much change. The Westbourne river and the lane beside it which ran from the Bayswater Road down to the Royal Oak had been replaced by a new street named Queen's Road. Along the Bayswater Road itself, forming the northern edge of Hyde Park and Kensington Gardens, had sprung up rows of stately mansions habited by the aristocracy. Parallel with Queen's Road, like tributaries of the Bayswater Road, had been laid out a series of terraces, Westbourne Terrace, Gloucester Terrace, and Porchester Terrace. And in the angle between Queen's Road and Westbourne Grove were several quiet and well-kept squares, Kensington Gardens Square, Leinster Square, and Prince's Square. It was a district obviously growing in prosperity, although fringed on the north and north-west by slums. Westbourne Grove marked more or less the dividing line between the rich and poor quarters of this new 'West End.' Inevitably the gardens along its frontage were built over and the cottages pulled down to make way for the houses of professional men and for shops.[1] But these shops seemed to confirm by their ill-success the warnings of the *Handy Book*

[1] The first shop in Westbourne Grove was that of a chemist named Holmes. It was opened in 1854.

of Shopkeeping. The rich people who were settling in Bayswater seemed somehow to continue patronizing the larger shops farther east—Shoolbred's, for instance, which made a practice of following up its aristocratic clients as they moved westward, and so keeping their custom. No one seemed to do any good in Westbourne Grove, and the number of empty premises always to be seen there soon earned it the nickname in the shopkeeping world of "Bankruptcy Avenue."

This was the spot to which Whiteley directed his footsteps in the course of his search. "Although it had been painted to me in the blackest of colours," he said, "I thought it rather bright." Perhaps he may have been encouraged by a curious coincidence. About a quarter of a mile from the entrance to the Grove, at the corner of what had once been a field belonging to a Mr Paine, stood a stone with an arrow rudely inscribed upon it. This stone, according to local tradition, marked the place where a knight of the name of Whiteley had been killed many centuries ago while hunting in the company of one of the Plantagenet kings. Whatever the truth of the legend, it was of a kind to attract the would-be shopkeeper: the neighbourhood might be a 'lucky' one for him. Moreover, there was another consideration, of a more serious character. On January 10, 1863, the first Underground Railway in London was opened. One of its termini was on the edge of the City at Farringdon Street, the other on the edge of Kensington and Bayswater at Bishop's Road. This Metropolitan Railway therefore linked together the City and the West End, as well as connecting up with the Great Western Railway at

Paddington. From the look of it Whiteley could deduce the likelihood that Westbourne Grove might in the near future become much more prosperous than it was at the moment.

On the next available afternoon he paid a second visit to the Grove, and this time picked out likely-looking premises at No. 31 (then No. 63), on the south side, a shop that in spite of having had two tenants, both of whom had failed, yet seemed capable of being made bright and attractive. Whiteley was astonished to notice the number of fashionably dressed people who were walking up and down the Grove. To make sure of this he stationed himself on the pavement opposite the premises he had selected, and stood there for two hours, from three to five in the afternoon, counting the passers-by. At the end of that time he felt satisfied that their number and class were enough to provide the necessary custom, and that he could attract sufficient of them into his shop during the two afternoon hours to pay his working expenses for the whole day. He resolved to take the plunge and open his business in the Grove at No. 31. He found no difficulty in securing a lease of the premises for fifteen years at an annual rental of £140. It took him but a few weeks to fit out and stock the shop for the sale of fancy goods, especially ribbons; then he engaged a small staff, two young girls to serve behind the counter and a boy to run errands, and was ready to open his doors.

He chose a propitious moment when the neighbourhood—and, indeed, all London—was in festive mood. On March 10, 1863, Albert Edward, Prince of Wales, and Alexandra, daughter of King Christian IX of Denmark, were married at Windsor amid scenes of popular rejoicing. Three days previously London had given the Princess a rapturous welcome upon her arrival at Gravesend, and the arches, flags, garlands, and streamers which decorated the streets which she traversed on her way across to Paddington Station were still in place. On the night of the 10th, after the Royal pair had gone to Osborne, bridal banquets were held everywhere, and the whole of the main streets of London from Marble Arch to Aldgate were illuminated with countless gas-jets, supplemented with old-fashioned oil burning in glasses of many colours. Shop vied with shop in picking out with flickering lights upon its façade the devices of the crown and the plume of feathers. The day had been a public holiday, and the streets were rendered impassable from dusk to long after midnight by the crowds that thronged to see these illuminations. But far away to the West, in the comparative quiet of Westbourne Grove, Whiteley was toiling away with his two young ladies, putting the finishing touches to his fittings and laying goods out upon his counters. For he had chosen the morning after the royal marriage for the first day of his venture.

In spite of his preparations, however, Whiteley was rather late in opening his doors that morning. Perhaps he was finicky in adjusting the window display of his laces and ribbons to his own satisfaction. However, the omens were propitious. For before all the shutters had been taken down the first customer appeared. A lady named Mrs Johnson entered the shop, and asked for an article out of the window. Then, in Whiteley's own words,

> I apologized for not having the shop open earlier, and explained to her that it was our first day, and she said, " Then

I suppose I am your first customer?" I told her she was, and she then asked permission to offer up a prayer, which she did. And ever afterwards we were the best of friends until her death. She was such a lady as one seldom meets, and I always had the greatest possible respect for her.

Whiteley's shop was an instantaneous success, which confounded all the dismal prognostications of his friends. The reasons were simple.

Customers were never pestered to buy things they did not want; everything in the shop was displayed to the best advantage, and everything was marked in plain figures. All goods were sold at a reasonable profit, and there was a conspicuous absence of glaring tickets with "Cheap" and "Great Sacrifice" and similar legends imprinted in huge letters upon them. Purchasers were never given an excuse for complaint, and goods were never represented as other than they were.[1]

The fact was that shopkeeping morality in London, except in the case of the highest class of establishment, was at an extremely low ebb. This was particularly the case with small shops in outlying places such as Westbourne Grove—part of whose bad reputation was due to the high prices and exorbitant rates of profit charged, and to the petty tricks indulged in by its traders. Not for nothing did the technical manuals of the day stress the prime importance of the moral virtues as pointing the shopkeeper's road to success.

Punctuality, cleanliness, the neat arrangement of the stock, the attractiveness of the windows, the absence of all absurd puffing, the early and regular opening of the shop in the morning, and the attention paid to every one

[1] *Fortunes Made in Business,* p. 96.

OPENING SHOP

From *Twice Round the Clock*, by George Augustus Sala

entering it—these are the secrets of the small shopkeeper's success against the influence of giant capital.

Judged by this standard, many of the Westbourne Grove shops deserved the competition which Whiteley provided for them. A pointed contrast was presented by the flattering portrait of the model shopkeeper drawn in the *Handy Book*:

> A man cheerfully rendering his best labour and knowledge to serve those who approach his counter and place confidence in his transactions, making himself agreeable alike to rich and poor, but never resorting to mean subterfuge and deception to gain approbation and support; frugal in his own expenditure, not trespassing unduly upon the interests of others; but so holding the balance between man and man that his conscience may not reprove him when the day comes for him to repose from his labours and live upon the fruits of his industry—let the public discover such a man, and they will flock around him for their own sakes.

Whiteley answered to the picture tolerably well. Indeed, we can suspect him of having thumbed the *Handy Book* to good purpose when we read in his scrap of autobiography his own " little bit of advice to shop assistants who may be looking forward to starting in business for themselves one day. 'Add your conscience to your capital.' " Morality was worth its place in the window.

Before very long Whiteley found his business growing. He engaged another girl and then another, until by March 1864 he found that he required to cope with his customers no fewer than fifteen assistants, a cashier, and a couple of errand boys—a staff far beyond the average size employed by Westbourne Grove shops.

Whiteley had begun by selling ribbons, lace, trimming, and fancy goods. To these he added in quick succession departments for the sale of silks, linens, mantles, drapery and dresses, millinery, haberdashery, and ladies' outfitting, gloves and hosiery, jewellery, furs and umbrellas, and artificial flowers. By 1867, four years after the start, all these departments were in operation. Every month the sales of each were entered in a book, and each year the accounts were made up to the end of February. No records now survive of the firm's accounts prior to the year 1873, but the monthly sales books go back six years earlier. As 1867 was in several ways a significant year for Whiteley, it is interesting to mark in actual figures the progress which had been made. In round numbers the sales effected by the different departments during 1867 were as follows:

Silks	£5700
Dresses (including funerals)	£5900
Linens	£3000
Drapery	£3000
Mantles	£2000
Millinery	£2000
Ladies' outfitting	£3000
Haberdashery	£800
Trimming	£3000
Gloves	£2500
Hosiery	£1000
Ribbons	£3000
Fancy	£1000
Jewellery	£2000
Lace	£3500
Umbrellas and furs	£1500
Artificial flowers	*Nominal*

The sales of the seventeen departments therefore

totalled about £43,000, and, assuming that the rate of gross profit was the normal 25 per cent. and of net profit 10 per cent., Whiteley must have made about £4500 out of that year's trading. No wonder that he was beginning to think about extending his borders.[1]

In that year, 1867, he took the lease of his second shop, a little higher up the street, probably No. 41; and shortly afterwards in the same year No. 43*a*. He appears to have been called upon to spend a considerable sum (£2000) upon the former premises, either by way of premium or upon alterations and fixtures. The total value of his leases by the end of that year he reckoned in his books as £2850. Whiteley encountered no special difficulties in leasing shops during these early years, most of the properties in Westbourne Grove belonging to small owners who could not afford to keep them long unoccupied. Once he had begun the acquisition of additional premises the process proceeded with great regularity. Each spring he looked round for some shop whose lease had expired or which was vacant. He would take it on, remodel it, expand an existing department or open a new one in the space which it afforded, and ultimately buy the freehold when opportunity offered. Here are some typical examples of these early leases:

Premises	*Yearly rental*	*Expiry of lease*
Westbourne Grove, No. 33	£140	1879
" " " 35	£140	1900
" " " 37	£150	1900
" " " 39	£260	1889

[1] It was in this year that he took into his service James Keith, who became his general manager.

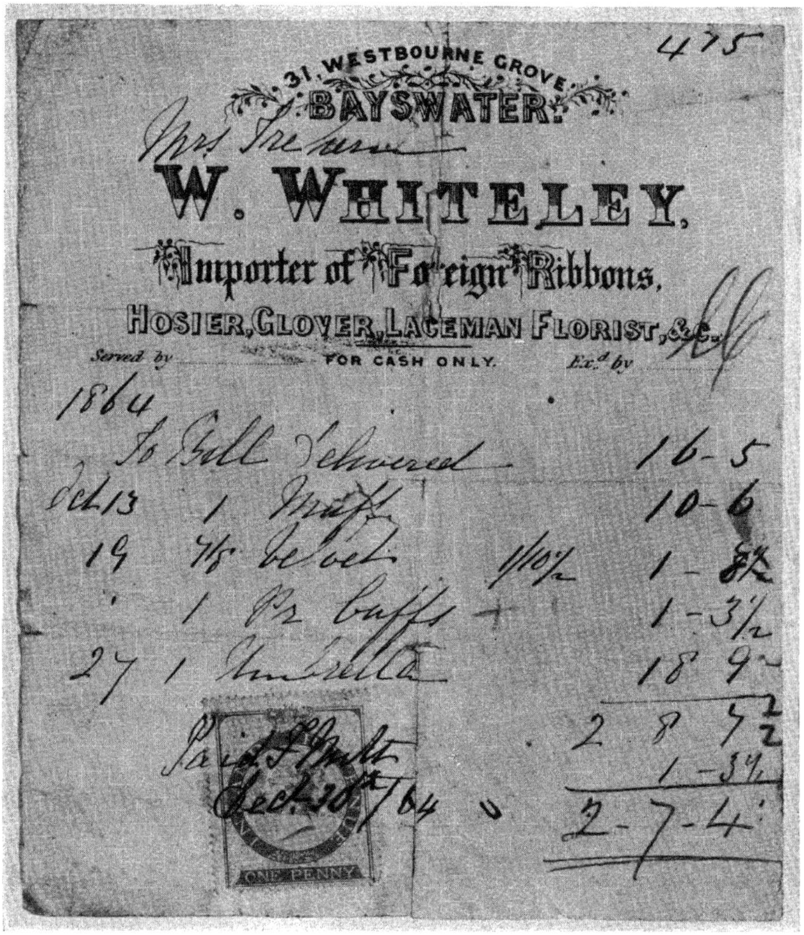

31, WESTBOURNE GROVE,
BAYSWATER.

W. WHITELEY,

Importer of Foreign Ribbons,

HOSIER, GLOVER, LACEMAN FLORIST, &c.

Served by FOR CASH ONLY. Ex.d by

1864

To Bill delivered 16-5

Oct 13 1 Muff 10-6

19 7/8 velvet 1/10½

1 Pr cuffs 1-3½

27 1 Umbrella 18 9

2 8 7½

1-3½

2-7-4

ONE PENNY

SALES BILL OF 1864

Thus in the course of a few years he came to be the tenant or owner of a whole row of shops between No. 31 and No. 53 Westbourne Grove. At first, however, he was cautious in the opening of new departments, contenting himself with rounding off the business of general drapery and clothing which he had commenced in such a limited form. In 1868 he undertook dressmaking, in the next year gentlemen's outfitting, then in 1870 costumes, in 1871 tailoring, boots, and hats, and in 1872 furnishing drapery. Several of these departments made phenomenal sales from the start. For instance, tailoring sales were in the first year of the department's opening £15,000, furnishing-drapery sales were £12,000, sales of boots £8500, and men's outfitting £7500. Thus Whiteley's appeal to the male proved as successful as his appeal to the female customer.

At the outset of this first period of expansion Whiteley took another momentous step, of a different kind. He married Harriet Sarah Hill, one of the two young girls whom he had engaged when he started his first shop. His bride came from Tufnell Park, and they were wedded on February 23, 1867, at St John's Church, Holloway. It was obviously a great advantage to Whiteley to have for partner one who knew the business and could look after his comfort and share in the work. For in those days it was all work, work, work, from seven in the morning till eleven at night or later. Long afterwards Mrs Whiteley described how she toiled and slaved on her husband's behalf.

> I married him just as he had taken his second shop and four years after he started business. What an ordeal it

> was for a young girl! We lived at the top of the house—and how well I can remember times without number sitting on the bottom stair holding a candle while he put up the shutters at night. Sometimes I could hardly keep my eyes open, I was so tired. Then we would go upstairs for a chat in our little sitting-room.[1]

It was not long before Mrs Whiteley had the cares of a growing family upon her hands. First in 1868 was born a girl, and then in successive years another girl and two boys, William and Frank Ernest. The arrival of these children, together with the extension of the business, made it impracticable for the Whiteleys to go on living in Westbourne Grove. Accordingly they took up residence in an unpretentious house in a quiet neighbouring street, No. 2 Kildare Terrace. Round about the growing family lived the firm's employees, housed in various lodgings on the then all-prevalent 'living-in' system. The bland, energetic draper ruled his staff with a sufficiently severe discipline; yet he could unbend, and had not forgotten his own sporting youth. He encouraged his young men to go in for games, and in 1870 founded for their benefit the Kildare Athletic Club. Thenceforward year after year he presided over its annual gathering, watched the various races being run, offered substantial prizes, and duly presented them at dusk amid cheering to the winners. And for some years he held every January a ball in a fashionable hall, to which he invited his staff and his friends. There two or three hundred young men and girls would dance a gallop, drink loyal toasts proposed in rotund speeches by their employer, consume supper,

[1] *News of the World*, February 3, 1907.

and wind up the proceedings with a Sir Roger de Coverley in the small hours of the morning. The spirit of the firm was paternal, not to say patriarchal; and its enterprise partook of the fierce, barbarian energy of its patriarch.

CHAPTER III

The Universal Provider

FOR ten years Whiteley had occupied himself with extending and improving his drapery business, but from 1872 onward he entered upon a second stage of activity, wherein he launched forth into new and unheard-of combinations of enterprise, going far beyond his original scope. Whiteley the draper became Whiteley the "Universal Provider"—a self-conferred title which he embodied in his trademark. He was drawn on to play this new part not merely by his own ambition, but also by the solicitation of his customers. Whiteley's famous politeness included an anxiety to oblige, which often took the form of going out of his way to perform a service or procure some wanted article which his shops did not stock. "Oh, Mr Whiteley," the gratified customer would say, "you sell us ribbons and lace at a penny a yard cheaper than anyone else. Why don't you sell us a jacket or a costume at a pound below what it is procurable for in Oxford Street?" "Ladies," Whiteley would reply, "it shall be done!" And he did it. His first experiments outside the field of drapery were the provision of one or two services to his customers—a house agency, for instance, and a refreshment-room, both opened in 1872, and in 1874 a cleaning and dyeing service. For his refreshment-room Whiteley had unusual ambitions for a shopkeeper; and he astounded the Paddington magistrates by applying to them for a wine licence, on the ground that many of his customers came up from the country to spend the day shopping at his establishment, when they would require of him "a glass of wine and a biscuit" to sustain their energies. Whiteley's application was put forward by his solicitor, Charles Mills Roche, of Old Jewry—a man of local standing and influence, a vestryman of Paddington, and the representative of the Vestry upon the Metropolitan Board of Works. In expounding his client's case Roche described the growth of Whiteley's business with the boast that "Mr Whiteley has been the making of Westbourne Grove." He now occupied ten shops, was rated at between £2000 and £3000 a year, employed 622 hands on the establishment and another 1000 out of doors, and served some 4000 customers every day, of whom from 500 to 1000, it was estimated, came from outside London. In spite of these impressive facts the magistrates refused the application, influenced by the plea put forward by an opposing barrister, who argued in the interests of business "that Mr Whiteley had got enough irons in the fire, and would not require any more," and (more quaintly) in the interests of morality that many of Whiteley's customers "might be ladies, or females dressed to represent them, and the place might be made a place of assignation."

This was the first check experienced by the Universal Provider, but it had no influence on his course. In 1873 he began to sell stationery, and in 1874 he profited from the fashionable demand for cheap Japanese and other imported fancy goods by opening a separate foreign department. Next he turned his attention to household goods. In one year, 1875, he started the sale and repair of furniture (cabinets), carpets, trunks, brushes and turnery, and china and glass. Two of these departments were outstanding successes from the start: thus in the first twelvemonth sales of furniture amounted to £23,000 and sales of china and glass to £9000. Then in 1876 he opened an ironmongery department, and began to undertake building and house decoration. Since Bayswater was full of large stucco-fronted mansions which required cleaning and repainting at regular intervals, the latter venture proved extremely profitable, contracts to the value of £9000 being secured in the first year. Also in 1876 wools ("Berlin wools") were reorganized as a separate department, and a hairdressing service was provided.

These developments necessitated considerable outlay on reconstruction and fixtures, as well as engagement of increased staff. When Whiteley bought a new shop he would have it redecorated, and if necessary rebuilt. Then he would establish a new department and employ an experienced buyer to manage it. This buyer would be responsible not only for stocking the new shop, but for securing a suitable staff of assistants to serve behind the counters. And as the number of employees multiplied the problem of their accommodation become more pressing. They could not live on the premises, and could not be kept in scattered lodgings. About 1873, therefore, Whiteley began to lease property in various streets adjacent to his shops in Westbourne Grove, first at the back in Kensington Gardens Square, and then in front in Hatherley Grove and Westbourne Grove Terrace. Here he housed his staff on the 'living-in' principle, men and women in separate buildings, or rather dormitories, for the employees took their meals in relays in dining-rooms in the basement of the Westbourne Grove shops. In that year he spent on his staff in all the sum of £26,443, about two-thirds of which represented wages and commissions, and the remainder the cost of 'housekeeping,' or providing them with food and lodgings. It is interesting to note that Whiteley cleared that year (1873) in net profits almost exactly the same sum as that spent on labour—that is, £26,000. By 1875 he had come to own the freehold of most of the houses in Westbourne Grove Terrace at a value of £12,284. By now he also held the leases of an unbroken row of shops from No. 31 to No. 53 in Westbourne Grove, as well as Nos. 50 and 51 Kensington Gardens Square. In that year too he penetrated into Queen's Road, which ran at a right angle to Westbourne Grove, his first shops in this street being opened at Nos. 147 and 149.

The feverish speed of growth of Whiteley's business during these years put him in need of all the spare capital that he could lay his hands on. His net profits were rising year by year, £26,000 in the year ending February 28, 1873, £36,000 for 1874, £51,000 for 1875, and £66,000 for 1876. No doubt much of this profit was re-invested in the extension of the business. But Whiteley devised another means of securing capital without the necessity of having recourse to loans or overdrafts from his bankers, Glyn, Mills, Currie and Co. He began to build up a little banking business of his own. Whiteley observed that many of his customers had formed a habit of doing nearly all their shopping in his establishment. They wished to pay by cheque for what they bought, so he encouraged them to deposit sums with him and to draw upon those deposits. His business was earning such profits that he could afford to offer the most attractive terms, 5 per cent. interest on all deposits, repayable at seven days' notice—and in fact the notice was not as a rule insisted on, but deposits were repaid on demand. These terms were better than those which most of his customers could get from their own banks; and so between 1873 and 1878 the deposits and current accounts held by Whiteley increased from £2400 to £32,000. This made a useful contribution to the rebuilding and enlarging of premises which went on year after year.

All these developments were regarded with dislike and dismay by the lesser shopkeepers in Westbourne Grove and its neighbourhood. They saw one little business after another close down or sell out and pass into Whiteley's hands, to be transformed into some new department of his giant store. This dislike was greatly intensified when he ceased to limit himself to the branches of drapery, entered general household furnishing, and offered services of various kinds to his customers. But it swelled into rage when in 1875 came the announcement of his intention to embark on a wholly new line of business—dealing in provisions. The butchers of Westbourne Grove were unpopular themselves; they charged high prices, marked imported meat as if it were home-grown, and employed other annoying devices. Whiteley saw his opportunity. New methods of carriage, storage, and preservation made it possible to import more meat from overseas and sell it cheaper. And so in the autumn of 1875 he opened a butcher's shop at No. 14*a* Westbourne Grove, and undersold by twopence or fourpence a pound all his competitors. At the same time he began to sell fresh vegetables and other provisions.

At once the critics found their voice, and gave tongue in the local weekly paper, the *Bayswater Chronicle*, which intrigued its readers by publishing the correspondence under the heading, "Wholesale Butchery in Bayswater—the Victims." The first protest came on November 11 over the *nom de plume* "Senex."

> I am one of those who have been watching how far the gigantic Westbourne Grove monopoly would go before it would call forth public remonstrance. I have now seen a startling succession of feats in the art of shutting up your neighbour's shop and driving him elsewhere; but this last daring and audacious feat—this vending of meat and greens as well as silks and satins—overtops them all.

The establishment of the new departments would be socially disastrous.

> A new and hitherto undamaged class of small and struggling people—costermongers and watercress girls, as well as small shopkeepers—are now brought within the arena of the Leviathan's victims. And perhaps when the public realize what unlimited and unscrupulous competition really means in accessions to the poor rate they will find that there is such a thing as buying in *too* cheap a market.

Support for the indictment brought by "Senex" was provided by a letter in the next issue from a small shopkeeper who claimed to be one of the victims. He had set up in business four years before Whiteley came to the Grove, not far from No. 31. Since then, he wrote,

> I have for a considerable time been under the necessity of standing behind my counter when would-be ladies and

> gentlemen come into the shop, find fault with my goods and charges, and finally tell me they will go to Whiteley's; and they go, wearing the latest new fashionable dress purchased for ready cash at the above well-known establishment, whilst their last bill with their small tradesman has remained unpaid for nine or twelve months.

There was, however, another side to this complaint; for in the same issue (November 18) another shopkeeper—but this time a wholesaler—put the point of view of "the other portion of the community who have been begging these many years for release from the oppression of the small shopkeeper." He himself had been a householder for twenty-two years, and had paid all tradesmen weekly, but had never been granted any allowance or discount, though he had often asked for it. He concluded:

> Is it then treasonable for such as I am to welcome the appearance in the Grove of a provision shop conducted on cash principles, where I find that I can at least get what I always knew that I was entitled to—*viz.*, value for my ready money in the shape of excellent food at 15 to 25 per cent. under the rates I hitherto have been charged?

The real trouble, as "Senex" explained in a second letter, was not so much that Whiteley undersold his competitors, as that through his much greater resources he could go on reducing prices until he was selling below cost, and could continue the process indefinitely, until his small rival was worn out. Hence

> Mr Whiteley does not fight his fellow-tradesmen fairly. The kind of underselling which is characteristic of Mr Whiteley is according to the received principles of business of the very worst kind. . . . Let Mr Whiteley for one moment put

himself in the place of his fellow-tradesmen; let him ask himself, "Am I doing as I would be done by?"

"Senex" might appropriately have phrased his appeal in Whiteley's own words: "Add your conscience to your capital."

But mere words produced no effect on the Universal Provider. He had to support him not merely the approbation of his customers but also the visible evidence of the growing prosperity of Westbourne Grove and its neighbourhood, which must be due primarily to the prestige of his own business. Even the critical *Bayswater Chronicle* could not help emphasizing the change:

> The aspect of Westbourne Grove this season in the busier hours of the day is a sight absolutely without parallel in London. Where else in London, or on the Continent, can one see such a well-to-do and fashionable throng in the same extensive thoroughfare? The palmy days of Regent Street are over, and as for Oxford Street, it has only one side, and that a very mixed one. The Bayswater boulevard can only be compared with King's Road, Brighton, *the* place for shopping, lounging, and promenading, where everybody meets everybody. Mr Whiteley's meat-vans certainly alter the appearance of the East End of the Grove.

But there was one quarter where the disgruntled tradesmen of the Grove might hit back. Paddington, within whose boundaries the Grove lay, was governed in its local affairs by an elected Vestry. Down to this time the character of this Vestry remained appropriate to what had, within living memory, been a rural parish—that is, the ratepayers elected landowners and professional men to manage their affairs. But as the parish became urbanized more and more tradesmen gained seats on the Vestry, until by 1870 it had lost its aristocratic and professional complexion and become commercial. It was on this body that the antipathy to Whiteley first began to show itself. In 1871 James Flood, a liveryman of the City, a member of the Company of Spectacle-makers, and head of a firm of auctioneers and estate agents in the district, had been elected a vestryman. Next year Whiteley opened his own house and estate agency, which must have competed with Flood's business. Within two more years Flood had come to the front within the Vestry, and began to take the lead in administering a series of checks to the upstart Universal Provider.

The initial opportunity presented itself when Whiteley took premises for the first time in Queen's Road—two houses, Nos. 147 and 149, which he proceeded to fit up as a warehouse at a cost of £1000. These premises were situated on the north side of Paddington Public Baths, which were managed by a body of Commissioners responsible financially to the Vestry. Of this body Flood, nicknamed "the Lord Beaconsfield of Paddington," was chairman. When Whiteley submitted to the Vestry, according to the building by-laws, the plans for his new warehouse—a tall building with many windows—he found himself facing serious objections raised by the Baths Commissioners. Their first complaint was that he was taking advantage of the fact that they had not yet built over all the ground at their disposal, to secure for his new building a "side-light," instead of going to the expense of providing it with a central yard and a "well-light." But Whiteley thought he could afford to disregard the Commissioners, relying on the fact that his solicitor, C. M.

Roche, was clerk to the Commissioners and also an influential member of the Vestry. He therefore adhered to his plan and commenced work on the building. As soon as it rose, a clamour made itself heard among the residents of Bayswater. A prim lady, Miss Emily Faithfull, wrote to the *Bayswater Chronicle* declaring that from the windows of the new warehouse the privacy of the Baths might be violated. And Miss Faithfull's protest was reinforced by a memorial from residents in Kensington Gardens Square who objected to having their houses and gardens overlooked.

The Commissioners seized eagerly upon this argument. Whiteley's Queen's Road warehouse would be frequented by Peeping Toms. From the windows of the upper story you could look right down into the men's first- and second-class private baths. Moreover, the new building might catch fire, and the District Surveyor had reported that it contravened the requirements of the Building Act, inasmuch as its cubic measurement indicated the necessity for more party walls, without which its many windows would, in case of fire, create a draught and probably involve the Baths in the conflagration. When the Commissioners called the Vestry's attention to this report the latter decided to send it on to the Metropolitan Board of Works, whose duty it was to see that the Building Acts were enforced. But here Whiteley had taken the measure of his opponents in advance. Indeed, he cared little for any appeal to the Board of Works, since two of his most powerful supporters, C. M. Roche, his solicitor, and Ebenezer Saunders, the architect of the criticized warehouse, were members of the Board—the former since 1860. In due course the Surveyor's report was received by the Board, considered, and then put back for reconsideration—while the work of building went on. At length the Board referred the matter to its Building Acts Committee, which decided that as the criticized building was to be used only as a warehouse and not as a retail shop action against Whiteley need not be pressed.

Thus baffled, the Paddington Baths Commissioners, led by the indefatigable Flood, fell back upon a second method of vindicating the rights of the parish. They proposed to block up the offending view and lessen the danger of fire to the Baths by erecting, opposite Whiteley's windows, a brick wall of their own, at an estimated cost of a couple of hundred pounds. In due course they approached the Paddington Vestry for permission to take this serious step and to incur the expense it involved. Whiteley, of course, was ready for the contest. He had obtained from Roche some idea of the arguments which the Commissioners intended to bring in support of their scheme, and was able to rebut the most serious of them—that relating to the increased risk of fire—by a simple device. Both his warehouse and the Baths were insured with the same company, the Royal Insurance Office. Whiteley wrote to the Insurance Company, showed them a plan of his warehouse, and inquired whether the erection would in any way increase the danger of fire at the Baths or cause the company to increase its premium. He was able triumphantly to produce to the Vestry the company's letter replying in the negative. But to reinforce the argument he also reduced the number of side-windows in his building. At length the Commissioners' request came before the Vestry, and was hotly debated, Flood leading the anti- and Roche the pro-Whiteley faction. Perhaps the suggestion made during the debate that Roche had misused his position and had showed Whiteley papers relating to the Commissioners' case before the Commissioners themselves had seen them may have turned the scale. At any rate the voting was even, but went narrowly against Whiteley. By a majority of twenty-six to twenty-two the Vestry decided to finance the building of the new wall. The decision was more of a snub than a real setback to Whiteley. Its chief significance lay in the fact that henceforth, for the next ten years, he could count upon the steady hostility of the party predominant in Paddington local politics.

During the following year, 1876, Whiteley's unpopularity increased steadily. He had allowed himself to become connected, in circumstances making for misunderstanding, with an unfortunate business venture launched by his friend Labouchere. This was a scheme for promoting a pleasure resort in Westminster to be called the Royal Aquarium and Winter and Summer Garden. Labouchere had the idea of appealing simultaneously to intellectual and to social circles. The company was to organize first-rate concerts and dances, and also to encourage the scientific study of plant and animal life. Shares were to be offered to the public in units of five pounds, each share certificate carrying with it a fellowship ticket admitting to the Aquarium. At first the shares were in great demand, and went to a premium. But soon the enterprise seemed to languish, and there was delay in getting the building completed and the institution opened. At this point

Labouchere, who was chairman of the company, appealed to Whiteley for help. The latter took up 1000 shares, and persuaded his solicitor, Roche, to invest also. Then "Labby" invited the Universal Provider to join the board of directors; and shortly afterwards the General Manager of the Aquarium, Robertson, approached Whiteley and asked him to contract for some of the remaining work, including the supply of refreshments. Whiteley agreed to oblige for a charge of £600, which was less than the previous estimate for the work, which had not been carried out. At last the Aquarium was completed and duly opened. But it did not meet with the success which its promoters anticipated. As the *Bayswater Chronicle* remarked:

> The idea of jobbing the second-rate aristocracy of the metropolis and the musical and artistic world as well, in order to attract the real spending public, was a good one commercially, and how it is that it has so far failed is a mystery.

But fail it did, and by the summer of 1876 the shareholders, whose shares were now worth only some five shillings apiece, became restive. Special meetings were requisitioned, Labouchere was shouted down, and Whiteley came in for criticism on the ground that he had entered into a contract with a company in which he was financially interested as shareholder and director. When it was shown, however, that he had only undertaken the work to assist the company in its moment of need, and had agreed to wait six months for payment, opinion began to veer round. Labouchere was formally censured by the shareholders, and resigned, but, said the *Chronicle*, "it is due to the Universal Provider to say that he leaves the Aquarium in good odour with both the rival parties—a sadder and a wiser man."

Meanwhile Whiteley's competition with the butchers and greengrocers of Westbourne Grove went on apace. In the autumn of 1876 he transferred his meat department to new and more commodious premises, which he opened on November 1 in the presence of a huge crowd assembled at its doors. The prices at which he sold both meat and poultry were lower than ever, to the rage of his rivals, who now openly demonstrated their feelings. During the whole of that week handbills were circulated "of an unsavoury character" throwing aspersions on Whiteley and the kind of meat which he purchased. Then on Monday, November 5, Guy Fawkes' Day,

> about the middle of the day, when Westbourne Grove was at its fullest, a grotesque and noisy *cortège* entered the thoroughfare. At its head was a vehicle in which a gigantic guy was propped up. This figure, evidently meant as an effigy, was vested in the conventional frock-coat of a draper; the mask (which represented nobody in particular) being surmounted by the ordinary black cylindrical hat. Conspicuous on the figure was a label with the words "Live and let live," whilst some clumsy epigrams to the same effect were pasted about the wagon. In one hand of the figure a piece of beef bore the label 5½*d.*, and in the other was a handkerchief with the ticket 2½*d.*—all linen! A company of butchers in blue smocks followed, making hideous noises with marrow bones and cleavers and unearthly cries. A rabble, who soon scared decent people out of the Grove, surrounded the actors in the unwonted scene, whilst the object of the burlesque stood at his own door, and surveyed the whole affair with apparent interest and amusement. The company having yelled and hissed

to their heart's content, the *cortège* moved on to make a tour of the district.

Later in the same day, after dark, the mob administered "summary punishment" to Whiteley's effigy in the Portobello Road, where he was particularly unpopular.

The Universal Provider no more allowed himself to be deflected from his chosen path by this outburst of trade jealousy than by a similar piece of spite manifested a few weeks later by the Paddington Vestry, which—as if to show him that his conduct in the Baths controversy had not been forgotten—ordered him at the beginning of December to take down the flag which he was accustomed to hang out across Westbourne Grove every Christmastide. "Mr Whiteley's way of placarding," commented the *Bayswater Chronicle*, "becomes the most hideous eyesore that an English visitor can look upon. We do not want to Americanize the Grove." But though Whiteley punished his critics by seeming to ignore them, some of his actions showed a secret concern to mitigate his unpopularity by more skilful propaganda. It was his rule, almost inflexibly observed throughout his career, not to advertise in the usual way in the newspapers. Doubtless this refusal raised his prestige with his customers; at the same time it left him exposed to the indifference or even the malice of the local Press, which derived so much advertisement revenue from his rivals. Not that Whiteley underestimated the power of the printed word. From the early days of his venture in the Grove he practised the art of circularization. He believed in personally approaching his clients by circular or postcard; in homely language he warned them every January or July of impending sales, or dispatched to them year after year an ever more richly variegated catalogue of the services he was prepared to render them. And in that autumn of 1876 he conceived a new method of publicity. He issued to his customers *Whiteley's Diary and Almanac for 1877*, which marked a new departure indeed in shop-keeping enterprise. The stout volume, bound in red cloth, looks dull enough to the eye of a later generation; but we can imagine the impression which its appearance must have created in many mid-Victorian drawing-rooms, with its compendium of practical information on weights and measures, stamp duties, and postal regulations, its *Whitaker*-like miscellany of useful knowledge, ranging from a Parliamentary directory to a gazetteer of places of amusement, and its spacious diary embellished with the feast-days of the Church and the quarters of the moon. From this autumn on for the next forty years *Whiteley's Diary and Almanac* continued to appear with clocklike regularity as the Universal Provider's Christmas gift to his appreciative customers.

The advertisement pages of the *Almanac* for 1877 show that Whiteley was devising for himself ways of evading his own self-imposed taboo on Press advertising. For while he refused to pay for space in the vulgar company of his rivals in the advertisement pages, he was not above procuring the publication of articles in the editorial pages, describing and adulating his achievements. His first trial venture in this field appears to have been across the Atlantic in the New York *Daily Graphic*, which contained in its issue of May 12, 1876, a spirited article signed with the pseudonym "Cathcart," faintly suggestive of old-world aristocracy.

There is in London a merchant—or, as the phrase here goes, a shopkeeper—who in thirteen years has built up a business amazing in extent and variety, and who if he lives a dozen years longer will probably be then doing a trade of the most appalling magnitude. This man is Mr William Whiteley, of Westbourne Grove, Bayswater. When I first knew his shops, seven or eight years ago, they consisted of four or five houses adjoining each other on Westbourne Grove, and were devoted to the sale of dress goods and haberdashery. But year after year he opened new shops, buying out the leases and taking the stocks of the former occupants, until now his domains are described as Nos. 31, 33, 35, 37, 39, 41, 43, 45, 47, 49, 51, and 53 Westbourne Grove and 147 and 149 Queen's Road—which is as if one should say twelve houses on Broadway and two round the corner of Bond Street. True, Westbourne Grove is not Broadway, but for shopping purposes it is quite an important street. The development of Mr Whiteley's business is a remarkable instance of what may be done by simply accommodating people. At this really remarkable place one can absolutely and without exaggeration have everything done for him. . . . Imagine, for instance, a successful gold-miner coming back to England with a plentiful fortune but with little else. He arrives in London travel-stained, weary, and without a home. All he has to do is to go to Whiteley. He can take a bath, have his hair cut, and be rigged out in fashionable garments to begin with. Then, without leaving the place, he can in a few hours be set up, with his family, if he has one, in a handsomely furnished house with servants, equipages, and everything handy about him; and to make him perfectly comfortable Mr Whiteley will take his money on a deposit account, give him a cheque-book, and pay him 5 per cent. interest besides. If he wishes to build a house Mr Whiteley will build it for him. If he rents one and wishes it repaired, furnished, and decorated Mr Whiteley will do that

WHITELEY'S WESTBOURNE GROVE PREMISES
From the catalogue of 1885

also. . . . And here comes in a very unique thing. Mr Whiteley will bury you, if you like, and erect a monument to you. . . . In a word, Mr Whiteley will take charge of you from the cradle to the grave, and give you your meals as you go along—if you can pay for it.

The picture is a startling one, Whiteley aspiring to be the Vicegerent in Bayswater of the Universal Provider who lives in the clouds above!

Timing it well, Whiteley launched his next essay in self-glorification in the *Essex Weekly News* on November 3, 1876. Here the rhapsodist sang the saga of a "Commercial Utopia" wherein "integrity, perseverance, and practical hard work have been the alpha and omega." "Thirteen years ago," began the article, in the style of Samuel Smiles,

> Mr Whiteley kept an obscure draper's shop at No. 31 Westbourne Grove. His establishment consisted of a trio, two young ladies and himself. But instead of neglecting business for so-called pleasure he devoted himself to his avocation, and ere long by sheer energy, administrative powers, and marked courtesy . . . made friends all over the world, made customers transact business with him, and has apparently met the Philosopher's Stone, and adopted the world-wide trademark of Universal Provider, a title which he richly merits. . . . Let us take a jog through this extraordinary block of buildings, this busy hive which employs a very numerous staff of clerks, and enjoys a postal delivery so luxuriously prolific that the morning 'postal' averages a collection of a thousand communications, followed by a delivery every hour. The opening of these employs fifty people, and a man, sometimes helped by seven or eight others, is entirely employed in stamping and posting letters.

The amenities of this Utopia included a telegraph office and post-office, directories and other reference works, all on the premises!

With the impressive information that "Whiteley buys pins by the ton" the enterprising journalist passed to a tour of inspection of the various departments. In the Gentlemen's Outfitting

> you can go in in one attire and come out in another, instantly equipped for wedding, garden-party, racecourse, funeral, or evening party, and, like the sheep in the child's song, leave your tails behind you. Should a sudden impulse seize you to visit India or the South of France it is all the same to Whiteley, who will accommodate you in a jiffy. . . . Hymen seems to reign in No. 37, and . . . the mysteries of baby linen may be learned by visitors to No. 41. In No. 43 lace, furs, sunshades, will be found: here also is Mr Whiteley's private room, handsomely adorned with paintings—and from this cosy hermitage amidst the rush of trade you pass to a spacious saloon set apart for the display and sale of furniture of all sorts.

On the other side of Westbourne Grove the journalist inspected the new provision department, and the restaurant where "ten kinds of soup are furnished daily, in addition to other numerous delicacies, all remarkably cheap." Finally, he concluded,

> we have not space to tell of the underground arrangements, nor of the thoughtful accommodation for the comfort of the 2000 persons engaged on the premises, not to speak of thousands off; of the great gas-cooking meters, nor of the multifarious arrangements, including a library, athletic club, dramatic club, volunteer corps, band, horses and stables, precautions against fire, nor the culinary arrangements for the army looking to Mr Whiteley for their daily bread.

Whiteley's artistic taste soon became the subject of ironic comment by his enemies. Thus for over a month during the spring of 1877 the *Bayswater Chronicle* opened its columns to a series of rather trivial letters called forth by the display in the windows of his furniture department of a painting entitled *Harlech Castle, North Wales*, by Sir Charles Leslie, R.A. Critics were quick to point out that the titles prefixed and suffixed to the name of the artist were imaginary!

> As there is not, and never was, a "Sir Charles Leslie," a member of the Royal Academy, this is rather astounding even for the Universal Provider. . . . Mr Whiteley's staff are decidedly shaky in their knowledge of art.

Evidently the offending picture was quickly removed, for within a fortnight correspondents were hotly debating whether or not the letters 'R.A.' had ever appeared on it at all; while rival tradesmen were seizing the opportunity to exhibit in their windows paintings obtrusively labelled "*Not* by Sir Charles Leslie, R.A." Absurd as this wordy warfare was, it was symptomatic of the aggravated state of feeling in and around the Grove on the subject of the Universal Provider.

Whiteley had used the handbill and circular and the sponsored editorial article to give himself the favourable publicity he needed. But, perhaps provoked by the continual baiting of the local Press, he now embarked on an enterprise which later he had good cause to regret. He attempted in March 1877 to establish a newspaper of his own under the high-sounding title of the *Westbourne Gazette and Belgravia Herald*. How little he knew about journalism and how poorly he estimated the skill it required is shown by the salary, two pounds a week, which he contracted to pay to the editor of his paper, Loftus Slade. The latter, when first summoned into Whiteley's presence, sought to dissuade him from his rash venture, and made the sensible suggestion that he would be wiser to spend his money on buying space in the *Paddington Times*. Whiteley, however, obstinately persisted with his scheme. Slade soon disappointed his employer in the performance of what he described as "one of the most thankless and unreasonable offices I ever undertook," and was dismissed from the position. Copies of the paper were sold in the streets or given away to customers—but in vain. At the end of six months the *Westbourne Gazette* ceased its undignified and unprofitable existence. Whiteley had lost £370 on the project, and—more serious—had greatly embittered the hostility of the *Bayswater Chronicle*. For the next seven years that paper rarely published an issue without some unfavourable reference to the man who had tried to rear up against it a local rival.

In the meantime, with or without the adventitious aid of such publicity whether favourable or unfavourable, Whiteley's much criticized entry into the business of selling fresh food seemed to justify itself from the purely business point of view. His butcher's shop yielded a turnover of £31,000 during the first year of recorded sales (1877); while in the same period the sales of the cheese department amounted to £27,000, and of the grocery department to £18,000. These very large figures show that Whiteley was meeting a real need among his customers by selling reliable food cheaper than the smaller shops in Bayswater. Similar success was achieved by the poultry and fruit departments, though an attempt to include vegetables in the latter did not at first prosper. Whiteley's decision to discontinue selling vegetables was a setback which tempted the *Bayswater Chronicle* to a sly dig:

> Mr Whiteley has renounced the greengrocery business, and there is joy among the costermongers and watercress girls. But the vendors of winkles are said to be uneasy. The large stock of pins which is held over in the haberdashery department must be a great temptation to the proprietor to embark in the small-shellfish line!

But while Whiteley was justifying his title as " Universal Provider " by the establishment of his provision departments, there is some evidence that his success in this field was reacting unfavourably on his business as a whole. The years from 1876 to 1880 were years of retrogression—measured by the figures of annual net profits. In 1876 Whiteley had reached a peak he was not to touch again for ten years: his profit in that year was £66,000. Next year it had fallen to £60,000, and in 1878 to £57,000; then there was a slight rally to £59,000 in 1879, and thereafter a heavy fall to £50,000 in 1880, which was actually less than he had made in 1875. During these years of retrogression, too, Whiteley hardly extended his enterprises at all. In 1877 he opened a department for silk costumes, and another for shipping goods abroad to his increasingly numerous customers in the United States, France and the Colonies. In 1878 no new department of any kind was started. In 1879 he opened an agency for the sale of opera and theatre tickets; and in 1880 he set up a department to sell waterproofs, and another to supply coal. The latter step he took in consequence of the unsatisfactory nature of the arrangement which had been in force for some years previously for enabling him to appear to serve his customers with coal. This arrangement was given publicity in the law-courts in a form which gives us both an insight into Whiteley's business methods and an estimate of the strain which he was feeling under the surface of his apparent urbanity—a strain which led him to find an outlet for his natural combativeness in a growing habit of litigation.

In March 1873 Whiteley had made a verbal arrangement with a coal merchant named Tassell to supply coals to his (Whiteley's) customers. He stipulated that Tassell should sell him his best coal three shillings per ton cheaper than the price other merchants were charging: of this three shillings Whiteley would pass on to his customer two shillings and keep the remaining shilling as commission for himself. Similar arrangements were to prevail in the case of the cheaper coals and coke. Whiteley was to supply the names and addresses of the customers, Tassell to deliver the coals, and the invoices were to be made out in Whiteley's name. The results of this arrangement were curious. In 1873 Tassell sold in all 1694 tons of coal, of which 641 were supplied to Whiteley's customers. In 1874 the figures were respectively 1914 and 712; in 1875, 2345 and 1208; and in 1876, down to October 6, 3087 and 2790. So it appeared that the supplying of Whiteley's customers had become by this time the greater part of Tassell's business. But in October 1876 Whiteley became dissatisfied with Tassell; his customers were complaining that the quality of the coal had degenerated. He therefore denounced the agreement, and arranged instead to obtain a supply of best-quality coal direct from the pits of Sir George Elliott through the latter's London agent. Then broke out a fierce quarrel between Whiteley and Tassell as to whose were the customers. Tassell sent round a circular describing Whiteley as his agent, and offering, since the latter had discontinued receiving his orders, to supply orders himself. This circular evidently infuriated Whiteley, who directed his solicitor, Roche, to send Tassell a fierce letter accusing him of "disseminating among his (Whiteley's) customers two deliberate falsehoods." Not content with this, however, the Universal Provider next printed and distributed 25,000 copies of a leaflet warning his customers against Tassell and repeating his accusation of falsehoods and misleading assertions. Tassell retorted by suing Whiteley for libel.

The case was heard in the Court of Common Pleas early in June 1877. To the disgust of both judge and jury it was protracted over three whole days by the obstinacy of the two parties, who refused to take the judge's hint and settle out of court. During the cross-examination of Whiteley the judge pertinently asked him, "Is it not a cruel thing to fight this, and bring the jury here again on Monday morning? Why don't you shake hands over it?" But at this the eminent Q.C. briefed by Whiteley, Sir Henry James, interposed, "My Lord, Mr Whiteley says he has such an appreciation and admiration of the justice of a British jury that this is a recreation for him. Mr Whiteley is willing to bear his own costs." So the case went on to its bitter end; and the jury, without retiring, awarded the plaintiff a farthing's damages. So Whiteley paid heavily for his 'recreation' both in costs and in reputation. Unfortunately, he had not learned his lesson, and indulged only too frequently in petty litigation in the years following. Vindictiveness in the courts was the ugly obverse side of his famous affability and politeness in his own shop.

Another lawsuit in which Whiteley was involved during 1878 and 1879 illustrated some peculiar aspects of his self-appointed *rôle* of "Universal Provider." Whiteley by no means objected to serving his customers in a personal capacity even in their private affairs when invited to do so. A gentleman named Bear, who lived in Australia, sent his son to complete his education at Oxford, and provided him with an adequate allowance. On completing his course at the university the son left Oxford for London, where he formed an attachment for a young woman named Montgomery. The young couple looked about for a house in town, and finally obtained one in Bayswater through Whiteley's agency. There they lived in a state of illicit bliss for three years, at the end of which time father Bear discovered his son's delinquency, and promptly sailed for England, meanwhile withdrawing the allowance. The young couple, finding themselves without means, pawned all their possessions, including the furniture in the house and some valuable presents young Bear had given to his lady-love, for the sum of about £120. At this point father Bear arrived in London, and summoned his son to meet him in William Whiteley's office. The Universal Provider had, in fact, genially offered his services as mediator between the enraged parent and his prodigal son. The result, after a discussion which we can imagine for ourselves, Whiteley embodied in a memorandum, according to which young Bear was to take the next ship sailing either to Australia or to Fiji (curious alternative!), and meanwhile to repair to Paris, while the house and pawn-tickets were to be handed over to Whiteley, who would take charge of them. Meanwhile Miss Montgomery was to be paid two guineas a week to keep her from starving.

Next day, September 5, young Bear handed over the pawn-tickets, accompanied Whiteley's clerk to the various pawnbrokers to redeem the goods, and duly left for Paris—whence, however, he soon returned without his father's leave. Miss Montgomery, when her pittance ceased to reach her at the end of three weeks, showed her spirit by writing to Whiteley and demanding the return of those of the pawned objects which belonged to her. When Whiteley replied, offering to let her have back either all the goods in return for a payment of £140 or none of them at all, she sued him and father Bear jointly for the withheld possessions. In Brompton County Court in December 1878 all the ingenuity of C. M. Roche could not serve to gloss over Whiteley's presumption, and the jury awarded the plaintiff fifty pounds and costs—a decision confirmed the following April in the Court of Appeal.

During 1878 the Universal Provider occupied himself mainly in consolidating his business. His success had naturally called into being competitors, who imitated his methods. He was fearful, not merely of old-established competition such as that of Shoolbred's, or of new competition such as that of Gamage's, founded in Holborn in 1878, but even more of the extension of co-operative trading among the well-to-do middle classes. The Army and Navy Stores had been founded in Victoria Street in 1871, and the Civil Service Supply Association a few years earlier. The latter even threatened to open a branch in Westbourne

Grove. Meantime an enterprising draper, William Owen, established opposite Whiteley's in the Grove, was actually trying to turn himself into a second Universal Provider. And not far off flourished another drapery, Ponting's, which had not yet moved from the Grove to seek new pastures in Kensington High Street. Under the stimulus of all this competition the rent of shops in the district was rising. New leases in the Grove were not to be had at less than £360, or in Queen's Road £200, a year—and this in spite of the fact that trade was none too lively at the moment, since the Grove was closed to carriages most of the year to allow of replacing its worn macadamized surface by newfangled wood-paving. To celebrate the return to normal conditions Whiteley heralded the Christmas shopping season that winter by pioneering with electric lighting. From 5 P.M. onward shoppers in the Grove were dazzled by the beautiful steel-blue glitter of a Jablochkoff candle, which reduced the adjacent gas-lights "to a dirty yellow glimmer suggestive of the worst of November fogs." The candle illuminated the roadway and the outside of Whiteley's windows, and nightly attracted crowds of sightseers.

The Universal Provider was already preparing for a fresh expansion of his enterprise. He possessed one block of shops in the Grove and another in Queen's Road. If only they could be joined together! To achieve this end he cast his eyes upon Douglas Place, a long narrow lane running parallel with and to the west of Queen's Road. If he could secure and widen this lane he would gain a magnificent approach to the heart of his rising emporium. But there were obstacles to his ambition; and one property in particular, described by the *Bayswater Chronicle* as "a sort of Naboth's Vineyard," cost him £13,000 to acquire. At length he found himself in control of the buildings on either side of that wing of Douglas Place which debouched into Queen's Road. Thereupon he employed Roche and other agents to prepare an 'improvement scheme' for widening the roadway by compulsory purchase; and this scheme was in due course fathered upon the Paddington Vestry as a public enterprise. Whiteley hoped that Roche's influence would be strong enough to push the scheme through, particularly when backed by an offer from himself to defray the costs involved. But the anti-Whiteley faction scented jobbery; and the equivocal position of Roche, who acted both as Whiteley's agent for the purchase of the properties and also as a member of the Vestry's Highway Committee, seemed to justify the suspicion. At any rate, the scheme came to nothing, and for many years the Universal Provider had to content himself with a covered bridge across Douglas Place, joining the two halves of his domain.

The setback—a real one this time—seems to have convinced Whiteley that he could not afford to let his enemies on the Vestry continue their campaign against him without reprisals. Flood and his friends were proud of boasting that Paddington had a "model Vestry" which set an example to all London in introducing improvements, such as the new wood-paving in the Grove. But improvements cost money, and already there had come into being a Ratepayers' Association, which grumbled at the rising rates and accused Flood of involving the parish in wasteful expenditure. Whiteley now began to support this association through the agency of Roche; and in the Vestry elections for 1879 an unexpectedly fierce contest was provoked in Ward No. 1—which included the Westbourne Grove area—leading to the displacement of four old members of the Vestry by candidates of the Association. But this was not enough to break Flood's rule on the Vestry: in fact, it merely stimulated him to make fresh attacks on Whiteley. He boldly applied to become himself a member of the Ratepayers' Association—and when his nomination, first accepted and subsequently cancelled, caused a split among its members he drew off his followers in secession and formed a rival but smaller association, which harried the main body.

Meanwhile the strategic loss sustained by Whiteley in the rejection of the Douglas Place improvement scheme became apparent when it was announced that he had bought up eight more houses in Queen's Road, this time on the other (southern) side of Paddington Baths, which thus became an isolated enclave within his growing kingdom. These houses Whiteley proceeded to reconstruct at a cost of £33,000 as warehouses and shops, which were to include a large market for poultry and eggs. At the end of 1877 he had bought himself what appeared to be a small country estate at Finchley, following the example of other successful shopkeepers such as J. H. Heal and James Marshall. But the Manor Farm at Finchley Whiteley regarded as a good deal more than a country residence for Mrs Whiteley and the children or a week-end resort for himself. He began to establish there a poultry farm and to grow vegetables on a large scale—all for the purpose, now revealed, of supplying his new shop in Queen's Road. And simultaneously with the launching of this experiment in direct supply he strengthened his position by widening the geographical range of his customers. He had noticed the success with which Shoolbred's had maintained its prosperity, even after its fashionable *clientèle* had moved away westward from Bloomsbury, by following up customers and delivering their orders in all parts of town. The Universal Provider, preferring not to rely wholly on the doubtful loyalty of Bayswater, planned to do even better than Shoolbred's by organizing a delivery service which would meet the needs of suburban and country customers as well as of residents in town. In his *Almanac* for 1878 Whiteley announced a delivery system which, for those days of horse transport and limited railway facilities, was a marvel of efficiency. Every day the London householder might rely on two regular deliveries, and the suburban householder on one delivery, by Whiteley's vans; while for his country customers the Universal Provider undertook to deliver and book free of charge at the railway termini parcels of goods which they had ordered in person or by post. In case of emergency London customers might even have goods, if paid for in advance, delivered to them by special express conveyance.

Expansion of enterprise seemed to call for expansion of publicity. As the Universal Provider looked round upon his work he burned to perpetuate its glories in some permanent record. He had already made one daring attempt to enlist the services of a man of genius. The favourite painter of the age, William Powell Frith, had his studio in Bayswater. There he had executed the commission entrusted to him by the Queen of immortalizing in paint the marriage ceremony of the Prince of Wales and Princess Alexandra in 1863. Royalty had visited Bayswater to sit for this picture, as they had visited Westbourne Grove (incognito) to shop at Whiteley's. Were not the Court painter and the Court provider therefore natural allies? Some such train of thought must have passed through the mind of the Universal Provider, moving him to the strange visit which Frith politely, but humorously, described in his *Autobiography and Reminiscences* as follows:

> A letter was brought to me, asking for an interview on "a matter of business," signed "William Whiteley." I was much puzzled as to what the "business" could be, as I owed Mr Whiteley nothing at the time; indeed, the principles on which he conducts his business are such as to prevent the possibility of anybody owing Mr Whiteley anything for an unreasonable time.
>
> Punctually at 9.30, the appointed hour, the great trader made his appearance, and a shrewd, smart, honest appearance it is.
>
> "Well, Mr Whiteley," said I, "I am glad to see you" (I was both glad and curious). "What can I do for you?"
>
> "Sir," said he, "I am an admirer of your works."
>
> "I reciprocate the compliment," said I. "I sincerely admire yours."
>
> Mr Whiteley bowed, and proceeded to say that he had seen *Ramsgate Sands*, and he greatly admired the variety of character, the—etc., etc. He had also seen the *Railway Station*, about which he was complimentary to an extent that my modesty prevents my repeating; and he admired so-and-so—running through a whole catalogue of my pictures—ending by proposing a subject for a picture, to be called *Whiteley's at Four o'Clock in the Afternoon.*
>
> "I should leave it to your discretion, sir, to choose either the inside of the place or the outside. If you take

the former you would have the aristocracy making their purchases. You might introduce the young ladies who do me the honour to assist in my establishment, many of whom are very pretty. Then there are what are called shopmen, with fine heads, and every conceivable detail for your back and foregrounds. If, on the other hand, you select the outside of the shops, you could introduce the commissionaires, who, as you may have observed, wear a picturesque livery created by me; you would have the nobility and gentry stepping into their carriages, with—forgive my suggestions; they are subject to your criticism—street beggars, toy-sellers—think of the contrast between them and my customers—and all the variety of character that Westbourne Grove always presents. There is but one stipulation that I venture to make, if you select Westbourne Grove for the locality of the work—namely, that the whole length of the shops should be shown, care being taken that the different windows should display the specialities of the establishment."

As I listened to this extraordinary proposal I found myself wondering if the proposed picture was intended to act as an advertisement for Whiteley's, when, as if he read my thoughts, Mr Whiteley said:

"I never advertise; I never spent a shilling in that way in my life. My notions of the advantage of advertising take the form of good things at so small a profit as to make the purchasers recommend their friends to come to my shops; and I have found that method of advertising so satisfactory that I feel no inclination to spend the enormous sums that some of my brethren in trade find, or think they find, profitable."

He then proceeded to inform me that he began in a very small way of business in a street off Westbourne Grove with only two shop-girls to assist.

"I married one," said he, "and the other—no longer a girl—is still with me."

I was greatly interested in my visitor, and sorry that an engagement with my usual ten o'clock model afforded me

WESTBOURNE GROVE AT 4.30 IN THE AFTERNOON

The scene Frith might have painted (see pp. 103–105).

From *Living London*

so little time to say much more than that I would consider his proposal and let him know the result. I thought the matter over, and declined the commission, and have often thought since that though I should fear to undertake it, much might have been done with it.

So the great scene *Whiteley's at Four o'Clock in the Afternoon* was never (to posterity's disappointment) painted by the brush of Frith. It was, however, painted in another medium—only a whit less vivid—by the pen of George Augustus Sala, most fashionable of mid-Victorian journalists. In the early summer of 1879 the *Daily Telegraph* devoted columns of its centre pages on several Mondays and Thursdays to a tour of exploration which Sala chose to make through what he called "Young London," but what Cobbett would have described as an enlargement of the "Great Wen"—that is, the new suburbs that were springing up to the west, north, and south of the Metropolis. We can picture to ourselves Sala, "black-haired, rubicund, with one queer, damaged eye (not wall-eye nor squint, and yet like both)," as W. B. Maxwell has portrayed him, hailing a hansom-cab and, with his "manner that was a blend of fierceness and geniality," telling the cabby to drive to the unexplored outer region of Westbourne Grove. We can picture him sauntering in his white waistcoat and scarlet tie along Whiteley's shopfronts, under the awnings which protected customers from the pouring rain.

Miserably wet as the afternoon was, I found Westbourne Grove crowded principally by ladies and by young gentlemen of that peculiarly bland and amiable type which points them out at once as young gentlemen who have not the slightest objection to going out shopping with their Mamas, their sisters, or their *prétendues*—especially with their *prétendues*. The next thing that struck me was the fact that the vast majority of the promenaders—under umbrellas—in Westbourne Grove were exceptionally well-dressed. The reason for this seemed to be clear. Westbourne Grove is less an artery than an organ. It is the centre of the new prosperous and refined district. I suppose there are fewer pawnbrokers' shops in the region lying west of the Edgware Road than in any other part of London. When you have passed the canal bridge there are absolutely no slums, and consequently no narrow and unsavoury little back streets pour into the Grove murky streams and beer- and gin-sodden, unkempt, and unshaven idlers, haggard or bloated slatterns, and ragged, unwashed children. A contingent of professional beggars may occasionally find their way on business-purposes intent to Westbourne Grove. . . . Otherwise the frequenters of Westbourne Grove appeared to me to belong exclusively to the well-to-do classes.

Quite and happily ignorant of the topography of the Grove, I looked around with inquisitive eagerness for my Whiteley. I found the name inscribed in tall gold letters over a large double-fronted shop on the right-hand side going westwards. "Wonderful Whiteley," I thought—it was a foregone conclusion in my mind that he was to be wonderful—"let us see what he has got to sell." I found his ample windows filled with a most miscellaneous assortment of wares. I found him in the shop on the right-hand side of the Grove, prepared to sell all kinds of groceries and preserved provisions of home and Colonial preparation. I found that he sold poultry, and that his green geese looked splendid and his quails delicious. I was very near buying a couple of his plover's eggs; only I was deterred by fear and shame from making the purchase. . . . Asparagus was also in Whiteley's line in the emporium of "the Westbournian miscellany." Also cauliflowers; likewise oranges. He was sumptuous in hares. I am not quite sure about his selling sausages, but I can speak with certainty about his being great in beef. The Dead Meat market in

Smithfield could not show statelier sirloins or lovelier legs of mutton than did the Briarean-handed purveyor of the Grove. I marked his sauces and his pickles too; his biscuits and his chocolates; his butter and his cheese. Altogether his show of comestibles put me in mind of Snyder's picture of *La Bonne Cuisine* and that grand kitchen interior crowded with "goodies" that David Teniers painted. . . .

But could Whiteley show me naught but edibles and potatoes? Was he only a Tyburnian Hedges and Butler? A Westbournian Barto-Valle? I plodded along somewhat sullenly to the extremity of the Grove, noting many shops and finding no more Whiteley. Novice, greenhorn, ignoramus that I was! It is on the left-hand side, where the numbers are odd—"there is luck in odd numbers," quoth Rory O'More—that Whiteley flourishes exceedingly. . . . The whole place is one great bazaar through which people do not pass incidentally, but to which they can go for a specific and definite purpose. I can scarcely imagine the denizens of Hampstead or Kensington or Hackney or Camberwell or Clapham resorting to Westbourne Grove save for the purpose which led me there—to see a wonderful sight. The Northerners would be faithful to their Shoolbred, their Maple, or their Meekin; the Southern *trasteverini* to their Tarns or their Atkinsons; the South-westerners to their Harvey Nichols; while for all and every part of the Metropolis a certain number of people on shopping intent would flock to Regent Street or to St Paul's Churchyard, to the Strand or to Waterloo House, to Piccadilly or to Bond Street. Westbourne Grove appears to me to have its own *clientèle*—to be mainly patronized and supported by its own denizens—those of the aristocratic and refined Tyburnia. But that the Tyburnians are intensely loyal, I should not be surprised to hear some day that Westbourne Grove had declared itself to be independent as an oligarchical republic, and with *Elle se suffit à elle-même* for a motto.

Sala's euphuistic adulation of Whiteley's emporium

roused savage comment in the columns of the *Bayswater Chronicle*, which made no secret of its belief that Whiteley had hired the journalist to puff him in the *Telegraph*. Grimly that July the *Chronicle* sounded to the anti-Whiteley faction on the Paddington Vestry a trumpet call to renewed conflict:

> Eight more shops in the Queen's Road doth the Universal Provider intend to possess, as if all the Grove and adjacent streets would in time be one shop and the shopman Whiteley—just as all Russia will be one prison and the gaoler the Tsar!

Hardly, indeed, were the old houses pulled down and the foundations laid of the new buildings which were to take their place than the enemies of Whiteley sought to cripple the new project. The Paddington Surveyor reported that the foundations were sunk so deep as to affect the draining power of the main sewers running down the centre of Queen's Road. The Vestry ordered Whiteley to alter his own drains, and when he took no notice of their order appealed to the Metropolitan Board of Works. But once again the influence of C. M. Roche thwarted the attack. The Board of Works sided with the Universal Provider, and refused in November 1879 to confirm the Vestry's order. Nor did it add to the sweetness with which his enemies regarded him after his victory that Whiteley chose this Christmastide to exhibit in his shop-windows the following advertisement:

> NOTICE
>
> Will be published, December 10th, 1879, at 15/–, an Indian proof portrait of William Whiteley. Size 24 inches by 18 inches. Arrangements have been made by which

these portraits can be sold here for 2/6 each, unframed. Only a limited number will be published, and orders will be executed in rotation.

[*Signed*] WILLIAM WHITELEY

WESTBOURNE GROVE
LONDON, W.

While the *Bayswater Chronicle* denounced the "extraordinary vulgarity of a shopkeeper selling his own portrait to his customers," *The World* asked whether the announcement was a hoax, or merely signified that Whiteley had gone off his head with success. The portraits, however, were duly exhibited, and Whiteley's enemies claimed that when at the end of ten days they were withdrawn from sale only four of the half-crown copies had been sold to the public.

The Vestry had found Whiteley's position impregnable so long as he had his solicitor to protect him. But suddenly that barrier against their attacks was loosened. For early in 1879 a City newspaper reported that Roche was involved in trouble over the bankruptcy of an ironmonger named Clark; that he had bought from the trustee in bankruptcy some insurance policies belonging to Clark at a rate below their market value; that the trustee had been removed, and that Roche had been compelled to repay the value of the policies in full with interest. The news caused scandal far and wide. A question was put to Roche on the Metropolitan Board of Works, which he parried by announcing his intention to sue the offending newspaper for libel. But the action, though commenced, broke down; Roche withdrew it and paid the costs. Then the inevitable followed, and on April 17, 1880, he was suspended from practice for two years at the instance of the Law Society. Whiteley, however, did not desert his friend, and continued to employ the same firm for the rest of his life. But the blow was an awkward one, as it removed the influence of a powerful ally at the moment when he most had need of it.

With Roche eclipsed, the Metropolitan Board of Works was inclined as never before to listen to the wishes of the Paddington Vestry. The attack upon Whiteley's drains was therefore renewed, as more of the new warehouses in Queen's Road began to rise. Ebenezer Saunders, their architect, was confident that even without Roche's support he could keep the Board of Works favourable to Whiteley, and in this view the contractor for the building, Brass, concurred. The Universal Provider was misled by their optimism, and disregarded for the second time the Vestry's order to carry his foundations no lower than seven feet below ground. Again the Vestry appealed to the Board, and this time secured confirmation of their order. Whiteley was therefore faced with the prospect of being involved in enormous expense, as well as in delay in the completion of his buildings. In March 1881 he appealed to the Vestry to stay its hand; but his enemies were inexorable. Rejoicing in their advantage, they began to extend the scope of their criticisms. Once more the old question was raised—were not Whiteley's new warehouses taking light and air from the Paddington Baths? More, was not their north wall going to repeat the violation of the privacy of the Baths that had already caused so much scandal in 1876?

Two of the new warehouses had been completed and opened in 1880. Amid rising public interest and speculation the remaining four, running a race with the progress of the Vestry's wrath, were finished in the spring of 1881, and thrown open to the public on March 24. They comprised a china and glass warehouse at No. 153, an ironmongery shop with showrooms 200 feet in depth at No. 155, at No. 157 a building and shipping office, with thirty desks that made it look like a bank, and above this a 'fine arts museum' of paintings and sculpture, and a large piano and harmonium department; and at No. 159 a huge provision department. Even the *Bayswater Chronicle* admitted that these premises presented "a frontage certainly superior to that of any retail house in the Metropolis." Each shop was furnished with plate-glass windows. In the basement was a huge cold-storage room filled with ice, the lining of the walls and doors stuffed with sawdust to keep out warm air. There were rooms for cleaning fish and trussing poultry, and a cellar filled with pipes, racks, and casks for wines and mineral waters. In Kensington Gardens Square a new refreshment-room was opened where all food was cooked by gas, and a lift was installed to convey food from floor to floor.

Much cared Flood and his vestrymen for these amenities! In April the Commissioners scornfully rejected an offer by Whiteley to buy up the Queen's Road Baths, in an endeavour to end the controversy, and round off his domain. Then in August the Vestry had before them their Surveyor's report that the depth of Whiteley's foundations had affected the stability of the Baths, which would now require underpinning. Worse still, it appeared that the upper floors of the northern end of Whiteley's premises were to be used as a huge dormitory for 300 of his male assistants. The building stood five floors high, and each floor had twenty-four windows. These would overlook the Baths —this time not the men's, but the women's section! In 1876 the Commissioners had built a high wall to protect one end of the Baths against the Peeping Toms. Now, five years later, they asked the Vestry for permission to build a bigger, better, and higher wall, to protect the other end.

As the *Bayswater Chronicle* remarked, "surely since the Shakespearean days of Bottom the weaver, Snug the joiner, and Flute the bellows-mender a wall never played so prominent a part." On August 2 the Paddington Vestry had before them the financial proposition involved by their anti-Whiteley policy. The Commissioners required £3000 in all, of which one-third was to be spent on underpinning the Baths and two-thirds on erecting a brick wall seventy-five feet high on the south side of the Baths, against Whiteley's windows. The sum was staggering to the vestrymen. It could not be raised out of the rates, and must therefore be borrowed; and a loan would require the sanction of the Local Government Board. The newly elected members of the Vestry who had been returned to press for retrenchment and economy were furious. For five hours the Vestry wrangled, till at last the minority was worn down by the constantly reiterated reminder that the ladies of Bayswater were ceasing to frequent the Baths through their fear of being overlooked. The financial resolution was carried by twenty-two votes to six, a decision reaffirmed at a special meeting called in October.

Meanwhile the Local Government Board appointed Inspector Hilliard to hold an inquiry into the matter before sanctioning the loan. Much of the evidence offered at this inquiry, which was held on September 3, was of a mirth-provoking character. Whiteley, "looking as bland as ever," sat listening to the Commissioners' counsel disclaiming any wish to impute pruriency to his staff as a whole, but reminding the Inspector that there were black sheep in every body. "It was hardly likely that many would pry into the ladies' swimming-baths or dressing-boxes, but the risk was enough to induce in ladies a reasonable dread of going to the Baths." It was true that Whiteley had offered to colour his windows with paint, fit them with bars, and have them all screwed down so as not to open, but "a man of prurient imagination could easily take a screwdriver in his hand in order to realize his desires," or he could stand on the sills and look over! Evidence was given that it was possible to tell from Whiteley's windows the colour of the ladies' bathing-costumes as they swam in the baths, and that one lady in her private bath had seen a man on Whiteley's roof peeping in through the windows. Pressed by this manifestation of modesty, the Universal Provider through his counsel offered to put up a wooden screen in front of his dormitory, and, when this compromise was rejected as not meeting the risk of fire, to contribute £100 towards a corrugated-iron screen. But the Vestry remained obdurate—Whiteley must pay a rent for light and air, Whiteley must pay for the underpinning of the Baths, as well as make the other concessions. All hope of a compromise vanished when the redoubtable Flood, finding that Whiteley's horses and vans used Douglas Place as a yard for loading and unloading, forced the Vestry to prosecute Whiteley, and succeeded in having him fined for obstructing a public right of way.

When the inquiry ended, therefore, Inspector Hilliard had an awkward task. He evidently thought that both parties were behaving provocatively and obstinately, and that there was much common sense in a petition sent in by 300 ratepayers protesting against saddling Paddington with the expense of building the wall in dispute. In consequence the Local Government Board took refuge in delay, hoping that the quarrel might settle itself; meantime the Vestry could not win sanction for its loan, and the wall remained unbuilt, while an interminable correspondence was exchanged between the authorities concerned.

Substantially, however, victory remained with the party that held the field; the Universal Provider had established the foundations and erected the buildings of his new shops in the way he wanted and in defiance of his enemies. The tide of his prosperity, which had ebbed since 1875, at last showed signs of turning; and the bad year which ended in February 1880, when net profits were but £50,000, was succeeded by an improvement in 1881 to £51,000 and by a mighty jump in 1882 to £60,000. The year 1882, indeed, was a period of record trading in most departments, as the following figures (which should be compared with the returns of fifteen years previously, already quoted) show:

Linens	£59,000
Ladies' outfitting	£55,000
Drapery	£50,000
Gents' outfitting	£40,000
Mantles	£49,000
Tailoring	£33,000

Boots	£39,000
Furnishing drapery	£47,000
Furniture (cabinets)	£67,000
China and glass	£50,000
Building and decorating	£31,000
Jewellery	£28,000

These were 'peak' sales in these departments for many years to come. In silks the 'peak' was reached in 1881 (£87,000), in dresses in 1878 (£97,000), and in lace in 1881 (£62,000). Millinery was comparatively backward, sales reaching in 1881 the comparatively low 'peak' of £18,000 only.

This return of prosperity was accompanied by a fresh outburst of new enterprise. The Universal Provider added to his list during 1881 nine new departments: pictures, pianos, florist, fish, wines and spirits, beers and table waters, railway tickets, forage, and hire and exhibition. Of these the most remarkable was the last-named. The hire department was the 'miscellaneous' agency which transacted for Whiteley's customers all those unclassifiable services which could not be assigned to other departments. The hire department undertook to equip ceremonies public and private, to cater for shows and entertainments, and to provide goods and services however exotic and extravagant. It transacted during the first year of its existence five thousand pounds' worth of business, and became responsible for most of those exploits which made the name of Whiteley legendary. Among those exploits the most famous, perhaps, was the supply of an elephant. The Universal Provider used to tell the story with relish to his friends:

> One morning an eminent pillar of the Church called upon me and said, "Mr Whiteley, I want an elephant."

> "Certainly, sir. When would you like it?" "Oh, to-day!" "And where?" "I should like it placed in my stable." "It shall be done!" In four hours a tuskiana was placed in the reverend gentleman's coach-house. Of course, this was a try-on designed to test our resources, and it originated in a bet. The Vicar confessed himself greatly disconcerted because, as he frankly avowed, he didn't think we could execute the order. He displayed the utmost anxiety lest I should hold him to the transaction. But I let him down with a small charge for pilotage and food only, at which he confessed himself deeply grateful.

Hardly less famous was the story of the second-hand coffin.

> Some one thought to have me by asking for a second-hand coffin. That was also a sporting bet. But it happened that at the time one of my workmen's wives had in her house a second-hand coffin, which she had received as a present from an eccentric gentleman who ordered it when he was ill and discarded it upon his restoration to health. The recipient, who lived in a very small cottage of a house, utilized the coffin as a cupboard for her bread, butter, meat, and suchlike. And the story having come to my ears, I at once purchased the thing and sent it on. But as a matter of fact I could have supplied a third-hand coffin if asked for it.

According to *Truth*, Whiteley duly turned the joke against his customer. Ascertaining that the would-be wag was giving a dinner party, he sent a cart up to the door, and before the astonished footmen in the hall could prevent it two undertakers marched into the dining-room carrying a coffin on their shoulders, and delivered themselves before the assembly of the following message: "Mr Whiteley's compliments, and he is very sorry he cannot get you a second-hand one, sir, so he's sent you a *misfit*!"

The hire department prided itself on being able to execute almost any sort of commission. One day, for instance, two music-hall stars arrived from abroad to appear for the first time on the London stage. Anxious to ensure for themselves a good reception, and consequently a good report in the newspapers, they arranged with Whiteley's hire department to pack the hall with a *claque* of persons who were to applaud each time vigorously. Other curious jobs undertaken by the department included furnishing subjects for a professional mesmerist and supplying a 'best man' for weddings.

Whiteley always had an eye for foreign visitors to this country. Victorian London was an inhospitable city for the stranger, and so it is not surprising that some of the shyest turned to the Universal Provider as their natural guide, philosopher, and friend. That uncouth Californian gold-digger whom Whiteley would undertake to look after from the cradle to the grave was no mere figure of fancy advertised in an American newspaper. He took real shape, as an overseas visitor, not, indeed, from California, but from South Africa. In the course of the Zulu War King Cetewayo was defeated by the British and deposed from his kingship. The ex-Monarch appealed to Queen Victoria for clemency, and in due course journeyed to London to seek an audience and beg her pardon. He arrived in London on August 3, 1882, accompanied by a group of followers, and the question of their accommodation immediately became an urgent problem for the Colonial Office. Who would undertake to house, feed, and guide a parcel of black savages, who might fall an easy prey to the vicious allurements of European civilization? The Universal Provider at once responded to the request of the Colonial Office. He received the King, established him in a furnished house at 18 Melbury Road, Holland Park, and entertained him in a fashion supposed to be suitable for Zulu royalty. At least Whiteley congratulated himself on having made Cetewayo happier than at any other time during his eventful life. He dressed the King up in a suit of fine blue cloth, a flannel shirt, and a brightly coloured necktie. In this apparel he used to receive visitors, sitting on a couch or throne in a well-furnished drawing-room. "We took care of him," said Whiteley subsequently,

> as if he had been a child. We anticipated all his wants. He had only one fault to find with the accommodation provided for him. No entreaties would induce him to risk his person on a four-post bed or in white blankets. But when the mattresses were taken off and laid on the floor, and red blankets substituted for white, his contentment was complete.

Cetewayo was an expensive customer to feed.

> When he first arrived his daily ration of 3½ lb. of beef contented him. Before he left his regular allowance had risen to 7½ lb. per diem. He clearly admired English beef. Cetewayo was very particular about his cooking. The beef had to be cut into steaks two inches thick, and cooked till it was as hard and dry as toast. Then it was eaten by itself. Cetewayo always made a separate course of every article of food. He would have beef as one course, sweet potatoes as the next, then beans and melted butter—and so forth. In drink he was particularly fond of champagne, although he had no objection to whisky. You know how eloquently he discoursed to a temperance deputation about the curse of intoxicants and his earnest desire to keep them out of Zululand. If his desire to keep rum out of Zulu-

land was half as keen as his desire to put champagne inside the corporation of one particular Zulu whom I knew well, Cetewayo must indeed have been one of the most zealous Maine law men on record. When he left this country he had added two English words to his native vocabulary. One was 'Good-night' and the other was 'Fizz'—and of the two he most loved 'Fizz'!

Cetewayo was received in audience by the Queen at Osborne on August 14, and his restoration was announced next day in Parliament. He left England on September 1 to return home. On the evening of the day when the King received the news of his restoration he was allowed by his "courier," the Universal Provider, more liberty than usual.

Whiteley describes the scene:

We had a small party at Melbury Road in honour of the event, and the quantity of food and drink that the Zulus got through was almost incredible. It was Fizz and beef, and beef and Fizz, all the night through. At last, when it was far past the King's usual bedtime, I insisted he must retire. As a climax to the day's festivity I made the King a present of a magnum of champagne. Cetewayo's eyes were fascinated by the magnum. "Why not drink it now?" he asked through his interpreter. "You have had enough; we will keep it for you till to-morrow."

"But if you leave it here *they* will get up in the night and drink it," pointing to his attendant chiefs, one of whom had commanded at Rorke's Drift and the other at Isandhlwana!

It was in vain that we protested we would put it out of their reach. "Let *me* take good care of it!" said the king.

"But you will drink it," we said, "and you have already had enough, and more than enough."

"No, no," he insisted, "I will take care of it; but I must take it with me to my bedroom; it is not safe elsewhere."

> So at last, after making him promise in the most solemn fashion a Zulu could that he would not draw the cork, we allowed him to carry it off with him to his bedroom. He went out of the room hugging the magnum as if it were a precious child. A few minutes afterwards, as I went upstairs, I saw the big bottle standing outside Cetewayo's door, drained to the last drop. . . . The next day it was not surprising to learn his Majesty had a bad cold, and could not appear.

Eighteen months later Cetewayo died in British territory in South Africa, a fugitive from his own people. But the vivid pen-picture of his London carousal, painted by Whiteley in a Press interview after the news had reached this country, shows that the Zulu King may be numbered as not least sympathetic among the customers of the Universal Provider.

CHAPTER IV

Behind the Counter

WHEN George Augustus Sala remarked that Westbourne Grove was economically so self-sufficient that it could, if it wished, easily declare itself an independent republic he was but stressing in his witty way the profound impression that he had received during his visit of a local life singularly rich, vigorous, and compact—a life whose continued vitality a generation later inspired G. K. Chesterton to write his *Napoleon of Notting Hill.* This district of Bayswater that stretched from the Paddington Canal to Ladbroke Grove and from Kensington Gardens to the Harrow Road was only a part—originally a suburban part—of Paddington; but it had come to have a unity of character as if it were a town itself, with a High Street in the shape of Westbourne Grove. This narrow, rather awkward street, which possessed few natural advantages and had sprung from mean origins, had become in a few years the rival of Regent Street as a shopping centre, and the superior of any other in London as a resort for people of wealth and fashion. We can picture it thronged with carriages and hansom-cabs, and traversed by horse-buses from the City and other parts of the West End, all bumping over its rather uneven surface (the Grove was often in the hands of the road-menders), and jostling the vans, handcarts, and pedestrians that moved along or across it, to a point of convincing the more nervous of its inhabitants that the

Grove was dangerously congested with fast-moving traffic. There were continual complaints against the number of vehicular accidents, and continual counter-complaints against the number of perambulators and dogs that choked both roadways and pavement.

According to the *Bayswater Chronicle*, in lament over the 220 people killed in the London streets during 1880:

> Perhaps the greatest complaint the pedestrian has against the drivers of carts and vans is the absolutely barefaced way in which they urge their horses at full speed over the crossings. At present a foot-passenger is no safer on the recognized and specially paved crossing than he is on any other part of the road.

Sixty years later, in the motor age, the words have still a familiar ring!

Christmas and spring were the seasons of the year when the Grove was at its gayest and most crowded. Then

> no lady who finds in shopping one of the pleasures of her life fails to make a regular pilgrimage to Westbourne Grove. The neighbourhood has an atmosphere of its own. Here shopping assumes the dignity of a cult. The pavements are generally crowded with smartly dressed women, chatting earnestly: it is all of prices, bargains, catalogues, and such things.

During the eighties it was an open secret that Queen Victoria and all the members of the Royal Family were regular patrons of Whiteley. The Queen had first discovered the Universal Provider when she used to drive up to Frith's studio in Pembridge Villas to sit for her portrait in the picture commemorating the Prince of Wales' marriage. She did not, of course, visit this or any other shops in person, but transacted the required business with appropriate ceremonial. Her commands were written down and transmitted by courier to the shopkeeper, who would then dispatch to the palace a special messenger with the goods the Queen desired to see. This trusty employee

> visits the Royal residence and sees a footman, to whom he explains his errand, and then is passed on for the examination of several other footmen, till at length by a series of stages he is brought into the presence of a lady-in-waiting, who takes his message as to prices and other details of the goods ordered, and also takes the goods themselves to be examined by the intending Royal purchaser. While the goods are being leisurely examined the messenger waits the Royal decision, be it a long or a short time, which is notified by a second appearance of the lady-in-waiting, who gives the necessary orders. The messenger then bows himself out, and is again passed through the hands of the different grades of footmen, till he at last emerges into the outer air of commonplace humanity, and wends his way back to the busy West End. Her Majesty is somewhat fastidious as to orders she gives for personal requisites. It is a well-known fact that should shopkeepers show these articles, or allow any description of them to appear in the Press, her Majesty would at once deprive them of her custom.

Shopping was not hedged about with so much formality in the case of members of the Royal Family. The Duke of Edinburgh made a practice of visiting Whiteley's every year at Christmastide to see the bazaar and buy presents for all the Royal children. The Universal Provider used to meet him at the entrance to his shop, conduct him to the toy department, and serve him personally. Again, Princess Beatrice used for some time to visit Whiteley's almost every week, and Princess Louise used to shop there incognito, under the name of "Mrs Thompson, of Kensington Palace." The most courteous and kindly of all his patrons, however, was the Princess of Wales, who frequently allowed her children—including the Prince who was later to ascend the throne as George V—to wander about for a couple of hours at a time through what was allowed to be the most attractive 'emporium' for children in London. The example set by the Court was followed by Society in general. Some shopped openly under their own names, others under a pseudonym to prevent recognition and flunkeydom: Mrs Langtry, for instance, patronized the shop under the name of "Mrs Levy."

The Grove, however, was not always peopled by fashionables following in the wake of royalty. There were times when it was invaded by a very different grade of shoppers—hordes from the proletarian backwaters of Paddington intent upon bargain-hunting at the sales. That the dignity of Whiteley's could be sadly (though profitably) lowered can be gathered from the *Bayswater Chronicle's* description of the January sale in 1881. The crowd has gathered outside the doors in the snow and frost.

> Says a Commissionaire in attendance, "The parties are most females, and they *squeedges* soft!" But, oh, the digs that *soft* elbows can give! And, oh, the clang o' wooden shoon—for which read heels—down the main passage of the shop as the bargain-hunters rush forward on their prey! The boot department, in which I found myself unawares, was crowded with at least four times its proper number, and as all the bargains were on the floor, such a game of hunt-the-slipper was going on as our grandmothers never engaged in in their maddest, merriest hours. There were mothers in Israel intent on securing school boots for their offspring; strong-minded females foraging for themselves;

> ma's of one syllable, and their tight-lipped daughters, dropping aspirates and picking up high-heeled shoes; and, lastly, a lot of youngsters, in their first decade, groping on the floor for anything that might turn up under their neighbour's skirts.

The heat was stifling. In the mantle-room "ladies, dauntless in the cause of dress, were charging into the serried ranks of jackets, dragging them off their pegs, and bearing them away in all directions to be tried on at leisure." In the remnant department the capsizing of counters sometimes led to scrimmages between vigorous campaigners whose boast was that "patience and a large shawl-pin work wonders in a crowd, and soon bring you to the front."

This was the seamy side of shopping. But even out of sale time the attractiveness of the Grove, like the character of its patrons, was liable to vary considerably. During the summer and autumn there were bad smells, and in winter thick yellow 'pea-soup' fogs to mar the fashionable parade. Now and again the scare of cholera would raise its head, and alarm the Vestry into improving its drains or purifying the water supply. Occasionally there would break out major scandals—a vestryman would be accused of corruption, a gambling hell or bawdy house would be discovered flourishing beneath the very nose of piety and snobbery. And while crimes of violence and disorder were almost unknown in the district, offences against property were only too frequent. Smart as were the regular frequenters of its shops, the Grove was infested with thieves and beggars, and the district was regularly disturbed by gangs of burglars. Pickpockets and shoplifters were hardly less of a nuisance. Most notorious was the impostor Agnes Clark, a tall, grey-haired, genteel-looking woman, who would single out some rich victim and apply to her with a pathetic tale of having been robbed of her purse in Whiteley's, and being consequently unable to return to her home in the country without the aid of a loan of her railway fare. Whiteley had to leave to his customers the task of prosecuting Agnes Clark, but he made up for this by the assiduity with which he pursued other delinquents, especially shoplifters.

The ballad *Ladies, Don't go Thieving*, which was hawked about London streets in 1867, indicates both the prevalence of the vice and the popular astonishment at finding it practised by the well-to-do:

Oh, don't we live in curious times,
You scarce could be believing,
When Frenchmen fight and emperors die
And ladies go a-thieving.
A beauty of the West End went,
Around a shop she lingers,
And there upon some handkerchiefs
She clapped her pretty fingers.
Into the shop she gently popped;
The world is quite deceiving
When ladies have a notion got
To ramble out a-thieving. . . .

Astonishing skill and impudence were displayed by these women—for Whiteley reckoned that for every male he caught 300 female shoplifters were detected. Though drawn almost exclusively from the middle and upper classes, they showed little of the timidity and helplessness we are accustomed to associate with Victorian womanhood. Whiteley, who had acquired through painful experience a detailed knowledge of their technique, once explained in a Press interview how they would hunt in couples, one woman going to

A SHOPLIFTER
From *Living London*

126

the counter and engaging the assistant's services, while her confederate, standing behind her, as soon as the assistant's back was turned would swiftly and dexterously whip the coveted article off the counter into some capacious receptacle. The long flowing robes which were fashionable at this time no doubt assisted their operations by providing folds and pockets into which stolen goods could be stuffed. But even so it must have been a physical feat of some strength for Mary Ann Harvey to stow away 24½ yards of velvet, 42 silk handkerchiefs, 2 pairs of gloves, and some ribbons about her person in 1885; Sarah Bennett 20 yards of silk in 1890; and Mrs Olive Magestie 14 yards of black silk in 1894. At the other end of the scale shoplifters were fond of appropriating small objects, especially tins of potted meat, pork-pies, or jars of Bovril—also toys, needles, and bits of ribbon. For all these offences severe sentences, usually several months' hard labour, were imposed by magistrates upon conviction. It was an age when stealing was regarded as a simple crime rather than as a psychological problem.

One of Whiteley's best stories was of a case of shoplifting which enabled him to play the *rôle*, in which he so much delighted, of domestic arbiter.

> It was discovered that three girls, the daughters of an eminent barrister living in one of the best West End squares, were continually taking things away from us without paying for them. Well, I thought the thing over. I did not want to be harsher on them than necessary. At the same time I felt it was my duty to let their parents know. So that same evening after dinner I went to the house of the girls' father, taking with me a private detective and asking for an interview with the barrister on some private business. Presently he came in from dinner, saying, " Mr

Whiteley, I know who you are. May I ask what I can do for you?" I told him as gently and as leniently as I could that I had every reason to believe his three daughters were dishonest, and that the gentleman who was with me, and who was the chief detective of the district, was ready to put before him any details he might require. The man grew perfectly livid with rage, and the only thing he could say for some time was a threatening "Mr Whiteley!" "You have done for yourself to-day," he said at length; "you are a ruined man. You shall pay for this as you have never paid for anything in your life. Go home and realize that the days of your prosperity are over, and that henceforth you will be a beggar. I shall come to your office at ten o'clock to-morrow morning, and I shall have somebody else with me. Perhaps you had better prepare for a journey, for I shall probably take you with me when I leave your office." And so on. I said I should be ready to see him at any time, and then we went away, leaving the man behind in a wild fury.

I shall never in my life forget the next morning. He was announced punctually at ten, and when I saw the poor man's face I almost wished I had been able to keep his daughters' misdoings from him. He was a self-confident, bouncing kind of man; but in those few hours he had grown old and haggard and depressed. He could hardly speak when I came into my room, and I was myself almost overcome by his emotion. "Mr Whiteley," he said, "I must apologize to you most sincerely for all I said last night. You were right, and I am deeply grateful to you for having saved me from a public scandal. I am going away at once with my daughters." He sold his house, forsook his splendid position at the bar, and left England soon after.

The increase in shoplifting was an inevitable corollary to the growth of giant storekeeping, and it was natural that Whiteley should do his best to stamp it out. But his methods were frequently harsh and ill-judged: his solicitor appeared to have instructions to press prosecutions home to the uttermost; and the recurrence of such cases as that of one elderly lady of good family who was forced to spend £300 in defending herself successfully in the Central Criminal Court against Whiteley's accusation of stealing one-and-elevenpence-halfpenny worth of ribbon merely increased his reputation for vindictiveness.

The extraordinary contrast between the two facets of the Universal Provider's character—his amiability to his rich customers and his harshness towards those who in any way offended or obstructed him—arose, perhaps, out of the necessity under which he laboured of making his shops a meeting-ground for so many different types, classes, and interests of humanity. Bayswater itself held two ways of living—that of the Lancaster Gate or Ladbroke Grove residents, with their leisured culture of lectures, music, and good works, and that of the Portobello Road or Notting Hill proletarians, occupied with their perennial struggle against dirt, disease, and poverty. Among the well-to-do there existed another class division, between the aristocratic, the professional, and the shopkeeping sections, who were separated from one another by an almost impassable social barrier, as well as by political and religious differences. And now among the shopkeepers themselves Whiteley by his success had raised a new division—between the small trader with a single unit of business and the big trader who added shop to shop and service to service. That this tendency was showing itself in other parts of London as well as in the Provinces did not soften the harshness of the blow to the small shopkeepers of Kensington and

Paddington. Nor did it please them to be reminded that Whiteley's growth had brought prosperity to others by making the Grove a place of fashionable resort, or that it had vastly increased the sum total of custom to be competed for in the district. For who could tell where the growth of his gigantic store would end? Would it not inevitably swallow up one business after another until a complete monopoly had been achieved?

Whiteley's adaptability in the face of so many problems perhaps explains the secret of his gradual triumph over his principal rival, Shoolbred's. The latter had been firmly founded long before Whiteley started business on his own. It possessed an aristocratic *clientèle,* and prided itself on the high quality of its goods. The business was larger in size than Whiteley's. Its location in Bloomsbury was hardly less convenient, so long as care was taken to follow up migrating patrons and secure the continuance of their custom by attention to their needs. Moreover, Shoolbred's prided themselves as being among the more enlightened and humane of London shopkeepers (in company with Debenham's and Marshall's, of Oxford Street) in the treatment of their employees. Discipline was not too severe, living-in conditions were comparatively comfortable, and leisure-time activities were amply provided for. The firm had, moreover, early fallen into line with the reasonable demands of the Early Closing Movement, and it was the boast of Shoolbred's that they had taken the lead during the early sixties in encouraging the Volunteer Movement by raising and equipping at their own expense a Volunteer company from among their own employees, to be commanded by one of the partners in the firm—a tradition honourably maintained till the Great War. Assistants who joined the Volunteers were given extra 'time off' to enable them to fulfil their military duties.

These virtues, which placed Shoolbred's in the forefront of London shopkeeping in the last quarter of the nineteenth century were, however, accompanied by some disadvantages which Whiteley was quick to turn to account. The aristocratic nature of the business produced a certain sense of exclusiveness, which only too easily took on an appearance of lack of enterprise. Thus the best advantage was hardly taken of the site upon which the buildings stood. The shops were grouped round the outer edge of a square, whose centre was only partly used, much of the interior block never rising higher than the ground floor. As Shoolbred's never developed a banking business of their own, all extensions and rebuilding had to be financed out of profits. No loans were raised for this purpose, but from time to time the death of partners involved the raising by mortgage of a substantial capital sum necessary to pay legatees. A contrast was also presented between the Shoolbred and Whiteley families, the former of which sent its scions (at the third generation, it is true) into the Army, Navy, and other aristocratic professions, while Whiteley trained his sons to succeed him in the business. In short, the rivalry between the two firms repeated in the sphere of trade the rivalry between aristocracy and plutocracy which was a general feature of society at the time. Whiteley won his victory by readier adaptability, greater enterprise, and a better sense of publicity. Shoolbred's took their stand firmly upon the high quality of their goods; Whiteley sought to combine quality with cheapness, taking advantage of the rise of manufactures on the Continent and in America to import goods which could be sold cheaper than the home product.

In person the Universal Provider was of short stature and stout build, of strong constitution and remarkable physical activity. His head was broad, his hair curly, his eyes grey and keen, and his complexion fresh. In later life he wore prominent side-whiskers, and his voice never lost its Northern burr. His bushy brows, piercing gaze, and firm, rather cruel mouth gave tokens of a masterful disposition, endowed with the power of rapid decision and equally rapid action. A female physiognomist, "Professor" Anne Oppenheim, gave during the nineties a description of Whiteley which the *Bayswater Chronicle* pronounced to be "by no means adulatory, and altogether a rather able piece of psychological analysis." This is what she wrote:

> The jutting-down of the eyebrows at their inner corner near the nose indicates policy and tact. . . The fullness under the eyes means eloquence, the faculty of verbal expression, suggesting that he is quick at repartee and would never be at a loss for a word. The thinness of the bridge of the nose indicates that he can spend money freely. The manner in which the nose droops at the end denotes reserve concerning his own affairs; also that he is rather incredulous, and would take little on trust. The elevation and fullness of the cheek under the eye suggest a harmless love of admiration, and that he is desirous to please and to gain the confidence of all with whom he may wish to deal. The facial expression is that of blandness and mirth: but he has a hasty temper, and knows how to control it. The width of the chin shows an intense love of nature and art.

Whiteley was by no means uncultivated. The walls of his private room at Westbourne Grove were adorned

WHITELEY SPEAKING TO AN OLD CROSSING-SWEEPER WHOM HE PENSIONED

From *The Illustrated London News*

WHITELEY WALKING DOWN THE GROVE

From *The Illustrated London News*

with paintings, some of which were valuable. "I am sensitive," he once declared, "to the appeal of the fine arts, and I qualify the monotony of business by resting my eyes occasionally upon the cool, refreshing simulation of breezy landscapes from the easels of our painters." He was also fond of music, particularly of opera, and was frequently to be seen during the later years of his life at Covent Garden. But his chief relaxations were to be found out of doors. Whiteley retained his youthful interest in farming and gardening as well as his passion for horses, dogs, animals in general, and sport. Every Saturday he would go down to his farm at Finchley to receive account of the progress of the week's work, and to view the state of the livestock and crops. He was fond of going to the races, and also of taking week-end trips to Brighton and other seaside resorts. He usually took his summer holiday immediately after the August Bank Holiday, when the rush of sales was over, and preferred the West of England, Devon and Cornwall—especially Newquay. From time to time business took him abroad to Paris, and occasionally to Germany.

He was an inveterate moralizer, always preaching to young people the virtues of frugality and honesty. But he was not the man to spare himself the toil which he exacted from others. Every morning punctually at ten o'clock he left home and walked to Westbourne Grove, running the gauntlet as he went of hundreds of beggars, whose importunity, he once estimated, cost him nearly tenfold what he would have spent if he had traversed the distance by cab. In later years Whiteley gave a pension to an old crossing-sweeper named Williams, whose pitch was at the corner of Porchester

Terrace and Porchester Gardens. Arrived at his office, he worked on steadily until seven in the evening, allowing himself no more than twenty minutes for lunch and ten for tea. He attributed the secret of his business success to his adoption of the principles of cash trading and small profits, and he was fond of boasting that he had never run into debt, and never sold save at a profit. He hated waste, and, believing that a use could be found for everything, gave his staff orders that nothing was to be thrown away without reference to himself. Towards the end of his career he formulated his business principles in a dozen simple maxims, thus:

1. Add your conscience to your capital.
2. Do unto others as you would that they should do unto you.
3. Do all in your power to please a customer.
4. Sell only that which will do you credit and give satisfaction to your customers.
5. Give the best value that you possibly can.
6. Humour your customers in case of complaint, even if your customer is unreasonable.
7. Mark all your goods in plain figures.
8. Be punctual in all your dealings.
9. Give good value, and sell for ready money.
10. Be punctual in paying your creditors.
11. Gain the respect of all those with whom you do business.
12. Be just to all—and show no temper.

Naturally such a man was autocratic by temperament. Even to his customers he could sometimes show the rough side of his tongue—as when he posted up in his new Queen's Road shops a manifesto declaring,

> It is perfectly disgraceful that dogs should be allowed to do the damage they do in this Establishment. If it goes on I shall at once prohibit them from the premises.

And a few months later the Universal Provider carried out his threat, without doing his trade that injury that his enemies forecast when they heard of the prohibition. Whiteley was meticulous in his attention to detail, and exacting in the standard of service he demanded from his subordinates. But he did not suffer from the common fault of dictators—refusal to allow in his *entourage* men of initiative and independence. His chief lieutenant was his General Manager, a dour Scotsman named James Keith, who had been with him since 1867. The head of the provision department—most important of all Whiteley's ventures—was Richard Burbidge, who subsequently started Harrod's and received a baronetcy. And several others of his employees in due course left him to start or manage businesses of their own which in turn became famous—such as John Barker's in Kensington, and the Army and Navy Stores in Westminster.

In the words of the *Bayswater Chronicle*:

> Wherever we go, Mr Whiteley's is the chief training-ground for heads of departments, who are afterwards nobbled by the stores all over London. They are at a premium, and premium prices have to be paid to get them away.

During the year ending February 28, 1883, Whiteley made a net profit of £62,000 (a sum only once hitherto exceeded—in 1876), handled in his banking department £78,000 of his customers' money, and spent upon his staff in all £108,193, of which about two-thirds represented wages, salaries, and commissions, and the remainder the cost of 'housekeeping.' Thus the days had gone by when he could expect to make an annual profit as large as his total bill of labour costs—a fact which may be taken as one sign of the gradual improvement which was taking place in the lot of the shop assistant. In order to assess the merits of Whiteley as an employer some knowledge of the conditions which prevailed generally in London shops is necessary.

From the end of the Napoleonic wars till the passing of the first Shop Hours Act in 1886 these conditions had been a scandal from which the world of fashionable shoppers carefully averted its eyes. The shop was not like the factory or the mine, where the treatment of labour could be investigated only by the inquisitive, reforming, or official outsider. A shop was a place of resort for the public, and shop assistants every day made personal contact with the customers whom they served. Yet while philanthropists and reformers busied themselves with shortening the hours of labour, reducing abuses, and improving hygiene in the factory, little or nothing was done to help the worker in the shop except through the painfully slow medium of the Early Closing Association. As early as 1825 the shopmen of the linendrapers, silk-mercers, hosiers, and lacemakers of London—some 20,000 in number—had petitioned their employers that fixed and rational hours should be appointed for their day's work—that is, closing in summer at 8 P.M. except on Saturdays, when the hour would be 10 P.M, and an hour earlier in each case during winter.

Then in 1839 an anonymous writer calling himself "Philanthropos" in a pamphlet entitled *The Linen Drapers' Magna Charta* pleaded for a law making it compulsory to close drapers' shops at 7 P.M. This was followed in 1842 by an effort on the part of some of the more enlightened employers, who founded the Metropolitan Drapers' Association to try to abolish the slavery of late hours. At that time shops seldom closed before 10 P.M on five days a week, or midnight on Saturdays, while more than half the shops of London were open on Sundays after 10 A.M. In 1847 the Metropolitan

Reprinted from the Advertisement Columns of

The Times

Monday, July 9, 1860.

EARLY CLOSING on SATURDAYS and the RIFLE VOLUNTEER MOVEMENT.—The following ladies have agreed to abstain from shopping after 2 o'clock on Saturdays, to enable trading establishments to close at an early hour, in furtherance of the Volunteer movement:—

The Duchess of Sutherland
The Duchess of Argyll
The Duchess of Montrose
The Duchess Dowager of Norfolk
The Marchioness of Westminster
The Marchioness of Clanricarde
The Marchioness of Salisbury
The Marchioness of Abercorn
The Marchioness of Breadalbane
The Marchioness of Londonderry
The Marchioness of Cholmondeley
The Marchioness of Stafford
The Marchioness of Kildare
The Marchioness of Drogheda
The Marchioness of Northampton
The Marchioness of Aylesbury
The Marchioness of Bath
The Countess of Shrewsbury
The Countess of Derby
The Countess of Ellesmere
The Countess of Warwick
The Hon. Mrs. Gordon
The Hon. Mrs. Hughes, of Kinmel
The Hon. Mrs. Montague Villiers
The Hon. Misses Waldegrave
The Hon. Cecily Stuart Wortley
Mrs. Petre
Mrs. Cavendish Bentinck
Mrs. St. Leger Glyn
Mrs. Grenfell
Mrs. Marjoribanks
Mrs. G. Glyn
Mrs. Holford
Mrs. Tait
Mrs. Ellice
Mrs. H. Herbert
Mrs. Tollemache
Mrs. Cardwell
Mrs. T. G. Baring
Mrs. General Wesley
Mrs. G. Bankes

EXTRACT FROM A "TIMES" ADVERTISEMENT OF THE EARLY CLOSING MOVEMENT

Drapers' Association changed its name to the Early Closing Association, and began to enrol a long and distinguished list of patrons, including doctors, clergymen, and public men, Charles Dickens among them. The Association eschewed anything in the nature of coercive measures or trade combinations, and concentrated on persuading shopkeepers to agree together to close at the same time. The Board of the Association consisted almost exclusively of employers whose establishments were situated in fashionable localities. The influence of its work was therefore largely confined to the bigger type of shop, and little or no impression was made upon the small retailer. In various districts the Association secured promises from a majority of shopkeepers to adopt earlier closing; but again and again the refusal of a small minority to agree to the scheme led to discussions among and secessions from the majority, until the ground gained was lost again.

The disappointment caused by this slow progress was voiced by Lord Brabazon when he wrote in 1883 that

> notwithstanding the praiseworthy efforts of the Early Closing Association for nearly forty years, it may well be doubted whether there are not now a larger number of shops open at unreasonable hours than when the Association first commenced its labours. It is common to hear of assistants who are kept at work for fourteen, fifteen, sixteen, seventeen, and even eighteen hours out of the twenty-four.

Some of the reasons for the divergence in closing practice between big and small shops were surmised by Jevons in his *State in Relation to Labour*:

> I venture to think that the early closing of shops in so-called respectable neighbourhoods is mainly due to the fact that richer customers usually go home to dinner between 6 and 7 P.M., and, owing to our *laissez-faire* system of moral legislation, ladies especially are obliged to retire from the streets about that time. The working classes, on the contrary, having come from their employment at some time between half-past five and seven o'clock, are then prepared, if not obliged, to begin their shopping. . . . Some doubt may arise as to whether the brightly lit streets of a poor neighbourhood do not really form the promenade ground of those who have few pleasures to relieve the dull, monotonous round of a laborious life. To those who live in crowded, dirty lodgings unsavoury streets may be a

breathing space, and well-filled shop windows the only available museum of science and art.

Reformers now began to direct their efforts towards securing restrictive legislation. During the seventeenth century an Act had been passed to prevent Sunday opening, and in 1846 Parliament had regulated the hours of pawnbrokers' shops. Then in 1871 Bank Holidays were established by law, and two years later Sir John Lubbock introduced a Bill to restrict the young shop assistant's working day to ten hours. The failure of this Bill to become law led to fresh agitation. A new body, the Shop Hours Labour League, sprang into being, which admitted employers and assistants to membership on equal footing, and demanded State interference, on the assumption that voluntary efforts had proved their inadequacy. But it was not till 1886 that the first Shop Hours Regulation Act was passed, providing that young persons under eighteen were not to work more than seventy-four hours a week. The hours of adult shop assistants were not restricted by law until the twentieth century was well on its way.

The president of the Shop Hours League, Thomas Sutherst, was therefore not much exaggerating when he claimed in 1884 that

> at this moment vast numbers of assistants of both sexes are being robbed of health, robust constitutions are being broken down, disease and infirmities of all kinds are being sown broadcast behind the counter, and death is daily carrying off the victims of long hours and overwork.[1]

The working week of a majority of shop assistants at this time ranged from seventy-five to ninety hours, the

[1] *Death and Disease behind the Counter*, by Thomas Sutherst, p. 2 (1884).

average being about eighty hours. A small minority, those employed in large establishments patronized by the wealthy, worked nominally easier hours; but even here it was not uncommon for the proprietors to take credit for magnanimity by pretending to release their assistants at an earlier hour than other people, while actually keeping them at work behind the counter, tidying up, mending, addressing circulars, or making up parcels, long after the doors had been closed. Several of the leading London shopkeepers gave evidence before the Select Committee on Shop Hours in 1886, and estimated the length of their working day as follows:

SHOOLBRED'S (700 assistants)

Winter months	8.30 to 6
Summer "	8.30 to 7
Saturdays	Close at 2 P.M. all the year round

MARSHALL AND SNELGROVE'S (550 assistants)

Winter months	8.15 to 6.30
Summer "	8.15 to 7
Saturdays	Close at 2 P.M.

JOHN BARKER'S (400 assistants)

Winter months (six)	8.30 to 6.30
Summer " (three) . . .	8.30 to 8
Other seasons	8.30 to 7 or 7.30
Saturdays	Close at 2 P.M.

SPENCER, TURNER, AND BOLDERO'S (650 assistants)

All the year	8 to 7
Saturdays	Close at 2 P.M.

DEBENHAM'S (400–500 assistants)

Winter months	7 to 6
Summer "	7 to 7
Saturdays	Close at 2 P.M.

These were the most progressive employers, whose conditions contrasted most favourably with those prevailing in little shops. The long hours were made more severe by the lack of adequate time and regularity for meals. It was exceptional for a humane employer such as Marshall and Snelgrove's to allow each assistant forty minutes for lunch and twenty for tea. In most establishments meals had to be taken—and rapidly consumed—when and as the pressure of business in the shop allowed. Said Sutherst:

> On one day ten minutes is allowed for dinner, on another fifteen minutes, and the very longest time obtained—to rest as well as eat the most substantial meal of the day—is only half an hour.

This estimate was corroborated by Inspector Lakeman in his evidence before the Committee which reported in 1892 on the working of the Act of 1886.

These long hours were usually spent "in small, low-roofed shops with an atmosphere laden with minute particles, and charged to the full with heated and gaseous impurities." The best-regulated and most spacious shops were not strikingly pleasant for any length of time.

> A ray of sunshine invariably reveals an otherwise almost imperceptible cloud of insidious dust which at every inspiration passes into the system. . . . Stuffs, calicoes, and silks cannot be continually torn, cut, or moved without throwing off clouds of minute particles, which necessarily impregnate the air of the whole shop. Purchasers of all grades in varying states of health come and go during the course of the long day, and the same air is breathed and inhaled over and over again by those who stand behind the counter. In the evening long rows of gas-burners help to use up what little freshness there is left in the air, adding

further impurity by diffusing heated nitrogen, until the place throughout is charged with a combination of gases which both irritate the brain and poison the blood.

The most exhausting feature of shop-work was the long standing. As Sutherst pointed out,

> Incessant walking for twenty-four hours was considered one of the most unbearable tortures to which witches in former times were subjected, for the purpose of compelling them to own their guilt, and few of them could hold out for twelve hours. . . . The shop assistant in these days is obliged to submit to the intolerable fatigue of standing for periods, varying according to the locality, from thirteen to seventeen hours a day.

There were, indeed, seats in most shops, but they were provided for the customers, not for the assistants. According to evidence given before the Select Committee of 1886,

> The shopkeeper imagines that if a customer were to enter his establishment and find a number of assistants sitting down behind the counter, an impression would be engendered that the shop was not well patronized and did but little business.

Assistants were therefore directed to pretend to be busy, even when they had nothing to do. Late in the seventies public opinion, roused by references to the evil in *Punch* and other periodicals, began to demand seats behind the counter. But, as the Select Committee noted, the reform was often rendered nugatory because those who used them were fined sixpence.

> One very large establishment boasts of the seats it provides for its assistants, but anyone found sitting down is reprimanded the first time, and dismissed on a repetition of the offence. The assistant, who worked there himself, added to this information that there were mirrors on all sides, in which every movement was reflected.

TAKING THE LAW IN ONE'S OWN HANDS.

r but Considerate Customer. "PRAY SIT DOWN. YOU LOOK SO TIRED. I 'VE BEEN RIDING ALL THE AFTERNOON IN A CARRIAGE, AND DON'T REQUIRE A CHAIR."

From *Punch*, July 24, 1880

The system of ' living-in ' was an almost universal feature of shop-life at this time. It had survived from a former age when journeymen and apprentices lived in their master's own house; but this domestic relationship tended to become transformed into a kind of feudal relationship, when the employees were so numerous that they had to be lodged off the shop premises, but in houses or dormitories belonging to their employer. Such a feudal relationship might be either fraternal and kindly or the reverse. Often it became a mere form of exploitation, whereby the employee was paid part of his wage in kind of a quality which he dared not criticize. The *Lancet* Sanitary Commission (1886) found that there were

> thousands of small shops in London where no sanitary accommodation whatever is provided for the assistant . . . They have to run out to the nearest public-house to find a closet or urinal. . . . They have no means of drinking water, so they have to drink beer.

Even in large shops accommodation for meals was often disgraceful.

> In one large grocery shop the assistants were made to take their meals in a dark basement, where the odour of drains pervaded the whole place. . . . In one of the branch establishments there was no closet for thirteen months.

The diet usually included meat once a day, but was not otherwise very nourishing or varied. According to the *Lancet* Commission, breakfast normally comprised " an apology for coffee, and two or three slices of bread and margarine "; dinner, one helping of meat, often rabbit; tea, a round and a half of bread and butter with tea; and supper, at 11 P.M., a small piece of bread, a small piece of cheese, and a glass of water. Often assistants were fed upon what could not be sold in the shop; for instance, a shopkeeper made a bad speculation in pickled pork, and fed his assistants off the stock for three months on end. A draper in the West End used to go regularly to the butcher just before midnight on Saturday, buy all his remnants or 'block ornaments' at twopence a pound, keep them on ice, and feed his assistants with them during the ensuing week.

According to Robert Jones, a shopwalker who had been employed in several of the largest shops,

> a man who in applying for a situation would dare to ask a question as to the accommodation for sleeping or for living would be at once set aside and told there was nothing for him. . . . We do not know what there is existing behind the scenes of a respectable house.

He recalled a bedroom in a shop, "a pioneer of early closing," which was infested with bugs and "terribly overcrowded," besides being dangerous in case of fire. Another assistant, quoted by Sutherst, declared:

> You will scarcely believe it, but it frequently happens that assistants who remain any length of time in the same house may have to sleep consecutively with over a dozen fresh assistants, no matter in what state of health they may be. It is no use objecting to so many strange bedfellows; you must either comply with the arrangements or leave.

Men assistants were often accommodated in large dormitories or cubicles, three or four in a room; women more often slept two in a bed, and up to six in a room. In one case a draper screwed down the window of the room where his female assistants slept; this was done to prevent communication with persons outside. Another assistant had the sheets of her bed changed only once in three months. Sometimes shop assistants were even expected to sleep under the counter. In the nineties, when conditions had improved, Booth described the accommodation of shop assistants as " something similar to that of servants in an upper-class family." Earlier the *Lancet* Commission had pointed out that the shop assistant had not even, like the servant, a kitchen to serve as sitting-room.

> Shop assistants have no residence, no home, but merely a room at the top of the house—sometimes a mere attic—where as many beds as possible are crammed in together. Here the shop assistant may throw himself wearily down and snatch a few hours' sleep; but this bare, fireless, overcrowded room is no home to him. Thus on Sunday, when the shop is closed, he must go out somewhere, and if he has no friends to visit, must wander listlessly about the streets or parks. These homeless wanderers may be noticed on Sundays in great numbers, especially in Regent's Park. On weekdays, also, between ten and eleven at night, the shop assistant is frequently driven out into the streets. The shopkeeper lives on the premises with his family, and does not care for his assistant or assistants to come into the private part of the house before it is actually bedtime. Yet what sort of walk, exercise, or recreation can a shop assistant take between ten and eleven at night? It too often results, especially when the weather is not fine, in his seeking rest and refuge at the public-house bar.

The long hours, the poor food, the lack of fresh air, and the absence of privacy all combined to render impossible any mental or religious culture or indulgence in the higher forms of recreation. The young men, parched with the dust and heated air of the shop, and weary with standing, too often drowned their fatigue and despondency in drink. The girls for their part were apt to think that anything in the world was preferable to the grinding toil of the shop, where it was simply "from bed to work and from work to bed all the year round." Girls like Kathleen H., who worked at the age of twenty in a fancy drapery in Ladbroke Grove from 8 or 8.30 A.M. to 10 or 11 P.M. and till midnight on Saturdays, with an average of fifteen to twenty minutes a day allowed for meals, and 'off time' of half a day (after 4 P.M.) per month, were typical victims of a system almost the only escapes from which were death and prostitution.

From a third to one half of all shop assistants were apprentices or young persons of both sexes under twenty-one years of age. It was a youthful profession—but only because those who followed it became prematurely aged and died young. Sutherst graphically, if somewhat melodramatically, describes the decline of young girls under the effects of such a life:

> The rosy cheeks and round full face speedily become pale and emaciated. The features sharpen, and the complexion assumes a yellow, unhealthy tinge. The eyes part with their lustre and show an ominous sinking and darkness. The expression loses its sparkling vivacity, and becomes stolid and sad. The legs swell, the back arches, and innumerable complaints supervene. Dyspepsia shows itself, the mind and nerves become shaken. The bronchial tubes become clogged, and the blood is speedily poisoned from the continual breathing of air charged with dust and impurity. A slight cough follows, which in numberless cases produces consumption, and, in fact, the whole system—mind and body—begins to wither and decay, evolving different forms of infirmity and disease, until the poor victim of this vicious system either drops into a premature grave or passes the remainder of life in bodily suffering.

According to the Select Committee of 1886, the annual death-rate of shop assistants between the ages of twenty-five and forty-five was 9·04 per cent.; while Lord Brabazon estimated

> that one thousand lives are sacrificed annually in London alone to overwork, and that three thousand to four thousand more shop assistants go back home to die. This loss of life goes on unseen and unsuspected.[1]

Few women over forty could keep their situation. The occupational diseases which ravaged their ranks included consumption, heart disease, indigestion, neuralgia, varicose veins, and disorders of the generative organs and functions. It was an additional hardship that shop assistants suffered in practice from enforced celibacy, since women at once lost their jobs on marriage, while (said Sutherst) " it is a thousand times more difficult for a married man than for a single man to get a situation."

This outline of the general conditions of life and work for London's shop assistants in the eighties provides a background against which we may set a description of the particular conditions that prevailed at Whiteley's. As an employer the Universal Provider was neither much in advance nor far behind the standard of his times. He was not a pioneer in early closing, or in any other movement for the reform of the welfare of shop assistants, nor did he co-operate during most of his career with fellow-tradesmen, or indulge in large charities during his lifetime. On the other hand, as the bigger London establishments shortened their working day and introduced other improvements Whiteley followed suit, and rarely made himself unpopular by standing out for a 'diehard' policy. During the eighties his shops were open from 8.30 A.M. till 7 P.M., and

[1] *The Cause of the Overworked Shop Assistant* (1883).

A WHITELEY STREET

Westbourne Grove Terrace, in which were situated the lodgings of the female staff.

From *Fortunes Made in Business*

closed at 2 P.M. on Saturdays. He refused to allow any of his employees to work on Sundays, and for this reason did not persevere with the establishment of a department for the sale of milk, saying that it involved Sunday trading. Moreover, he allowed his assistants fair holiday conditions; those who were engaged prior to March 1 were entitled to two weeks', and those engaged prior to May 1 to one week's holiday during the summer. Most drapers only allowed a holiday after twelve months' service.

The living-in conditions were also above the average. Whiteley housed his male employees in big dormitories at one end of his Queen's Road premises, and his female employees in lodgings in two short *cul-de-sac* streets leading out of the north side of Westbourne Grove—that is, Hatherley Grove and Westbourne Grove Terrace. These streets came to be entirely occupied by Whiteley's staff; and it was an amusing sight to see the young girls, wrapped in shawls, run from their lodgings to the shop, which they must enter by eight each morning, in time for breakfast before beginning the day's work. Anyone who was more than five minutes late was fined sixpence. In the lodgings every bedroom was shared by two or three girls, each of whom was provided with a feather-bed, a washstand, and a chest of drawers. The floor was carpeted, but there was no room for chairs. The bedrooms served as sitting-rooms, except on Sundays, when they had to be vacated.

The diet was above the usual standard. In the words of one of Whiteley's assistants,

> The dining-rooms at Westbourne Grove compare favourably with those of any other large house in London, and the comfort of the assistants who make use of them

> is much studied, even to the substitution of electric light for gas. . . . In each dining-room there are from five to ten tables; each table is presided over by a professional carver, assisted by a waiter in a neat, clean uniform, and the meals are served with lightning-like rapidity—five minutes sufficing to supply the wants of the whole table. There are different joints on almost every table, and an assistant may send the waiter to any part of the room for a cut from the joint of his fancy. . . . Each assistant is allowed a pint of good beer for dinner, and another for supper. There are no calls upon him to serve customers during dinner hours. . . . There are fresh joints for each party, and they are served smoking-hot from the ovens.

The main drawback was the long distance which had to be traversed from the shop to the dining-rooms.

> I have often begun my journey to dinner with a good appetite, which had quite disappeared by the time I reached the dining-rooms. . . . The smells were not pleasant, or conducive to appetite.

Another creditable feature of the establishment was the encouragement which Whiteley gave his employees to engage in various forms of leisure-time activity, especially out of doors. Most of these activities were carried on by clubs, labelled with the generic title of "Kildare," from the street in which Whiteley himself lived. The Universal Provider acted as patron of each club, usually presided at its annual function, and presented prizes of plate to be competed for. The Kildare Athletic Club was the oldest, formed in 1870. Whiteley took a special interest in its activities, and often directed that the best athletes when in training should receive an extra chop or steak with their midday meal. His enemies used to complain that he made the prize-giving into a means of publicity for himself by exhibiting the plate in one of his windows for a week before the annual sports. The Kildare Rowing Club was founded in 1877, when its first row was marred by the accidental death by drowning of one of the casual spectators, who was knocked into the water by a boat which was being carried back to the boathouse.

These sporting societies, which were provided by Whiteley with their own grounds at Acton, used to compete with similar societies organized by other leading shopkeepers, and a rivalry grew up between them rather like the rivalry between the 'houses' in a public school. In these matters, indeed, Whiteley's relation to his staff was not at all unlike that of a stern, but enthusiastic, schoolmaster towards his pupils.

A similar provision was made for indoor activities. The Kildare Library in Westbourne Grove was opened by Whiteley in June 1875 for his employees; but they had to pay for what use they made of its several thousand volumes, inasmuch as sixpence was deducted every month from their wages for the purpose. Besides books Whiteley encouraged music. The Kildare Musical Union gave its first concert in 1885, and for a long time was criticized in the local Press for the unequal quality of its performances. In 1896 a Choral Society was added; and there was also a Dramatic Society, which gave frequent performances of popular plays. In 1888 the various recreational activities were co-ordinated and given a building of their own, called the Hatherley Institute, of which Whiteley acted as President and Keith as Vice-President. The membership of all the clubs at this time amounted to about six hundred, or, say, one in every four or five of the total number of employees.

The wages of Whiteley's employees during the eighties

cannot be stated with exactness. A female assistant might expect to receive twenty or twenty-five pounds and a male from forty to fifty pounds a year—in addition to the provision of board and lodging. Many assistants earned commissions on sales as well, and the scale at which the heads of departments were remunerated can be guessed at from the fact that the manager of the hire department received in 1899 a salary of £400, and earned about as much again by way of commissions. Besides the library subscription two other compulsory deductions from wages were made—of sixpence a month for shoe-cleaning and of sixpence a month for the doctor. Whiteley's, like other big shops, had its own 'house doctor,' appointed by the firm and paid out of these regular contributions levied on the employees. This system was unpopular with the latter, and after one or two scandals had been brought to light (none at Whiteley's, however) provision was made for the employees to elect their own doctor.

Undoubtedly the feature of life at Whiteley's which excited most discontent and criticism was the severe discipline. Many of the employees testified to the contrast between the bland and fatherly demeanour of the Universal Provider when first engaging a newcomer and the harsh and relentless fashion in which he would punish mistakes or dismiss offenders. Every employee was required upon joining the firm to sign a form of engagement under which no notice for terminating service was required on either side. He or she could be dismissed, or could leave, at a moment's notice. Once or twice employees summarily dismissed in this way sued Whiteley, but as a rule the courts upheld the validity of the engagement form, provided no technicality had been overlooked. So in practice an employee was entirely at the mercy of his employer. At the time when he was engaged he was handed a copy of the firm's rule-book. "I think you will admit," complained a discontented ex-employee who wrote to the Press about it in 1887,

> that a more remarkable set of rules were never imposed upon servants by the arbitrary will of a master. These rules are 176 in number. . . . They are classed under fifteen heads, and provide an immense variety of fines for the violation of each rule—fines varying from sixpence, which is the least, to two and six, which is the highest. The last rule is that every mistake not before-mentioned in the 175 previous rules shall also be punished by a fine of sixpence.

Fines were imposed for arriving late at work, being untidy in bedroom or shop, staying out late at night without leave, going into another's bedroom, and such other trivial offences. These fines went, not to any charity or to any fund for the general welfare of the employees, but into Whiteley's own pocket; and there were some who claimed that there were cases where fines had swallowed up the whole of a delinquent's monthly wages. Though other employees found it easy to avoid being fined at all over long periods of service, the grand total of fines must have been large, inasmuch as they required a separate fines department, occupying up to seven clerks, to collect them. And the galling nature of the fines themselves was accentuated by a practice which prevailed of posting up on a large green baize board in the dining-hall a daily list of offenders, giving names and departments, the amount of the fines, the nature of the offences, and sometimes also cutting comments of a personal nature.

Fines and summary dismissal were the chief punishments inflicted for infraction of discipline. In their liability to these punishments the staff were at the mercy of two forces, one outside and one inside the building. The evil system prevailed of inviting customers to express their complaints by writing letters privately to Whiteley himself. Consequently any customer who felt himself aggrieved against a particular assistant could make the latter the victim of a secret denunciation to his employer. These letters were given every morning to a senior official to investigate, and at 2.30 P.M., immediately after dinner-time, the parties involved used to be summoned up to Whiteley's own office, where judgment would be pronounced, often resulting in two or three instant dismissals. Inside the building the rank and file of assistants were largely dependent on the goodwill and sense of justice of the buyers, who were set over them at the head of each department. Though the buyers could not dismiss on their own responsibility, to them was left the selection of staff marked down for dismissal at those periods of the year when seasonal reductions in staff were made. Twice a year, in January and July, came the sales, each of which would be succeeded by a period of slack trade. On the last day of each sale notices of dismissal were sent out to the individuals affected, but not until within half an hour or so of closing-time. As the sales ended on a Saturday, and as the dismissed employee had to vacate his or her room the same evening, Saturday afternoon was a time of fear and foreboding for a large proportion of the staff. By their right to select those to be marked for dismissal on these occasions the buyers exercised an unwholesome power, all the worse inasmuch as they themselves were rarely in those days persons of culture or understanding, but more often assistants promoted from the ranks, who had not been trained to avoid favouritism and bias.

The large number of legal prosecutions brought by Whiteley against individual employees is evidence either that the Universal Provider was excessively harsh or that the atmosphere in which his employees worked was demoralizing. His network of sporting and recreational facilities did not prevent the setting up in Westbourne Grove of a gambling saloon called the Monmouth Club, which largely recruited its membership from Whiteley's staff, and was only suppressed in 1881 after three years' lurid life, as the result of being pilloried in *Truth*, and of a libel action in which the principal witnesses were five young convicts serving sentences of imprisonment for embezzling from Whiteley. These five youths had conspired with a discharged salesman to steal money and goods from their employer and sell them to a receiver. One succeeded in robbing him of £350, a second stole bales of satin, while a third sent twelve pounds' worth of postage stamps out of the building in one week. Another large-scale fraud was discovered in 1886, when a combination of young assistants defrauded Whiteley of large sums by manipulating documents and altering duplicates. Next year another young man was imprisoned for recouping himself for his losses through fines by systematically stealing equivalent sums. Then in 1889 an employee of seven years' standing was sentenced for pawning thirty pounds' worth of silk goods and forging corresponding entries in his books. And in the same year a ledger clerk was found to have concerted with his wife a scheme whereby the latter bought provisions at Whiteley's and resold them elsewhere, while he intercepted the vouchers for the sales and destroyed them. By contrast with these elaborate and serious robberies there were countless petty pilferings, against the perpetrators of which Whiteley pressed home legal proceedings with a ruthless disregard of any extenuating circumstances. Thus in 1889 a carver in the provisions department received a sentence of six weeks' imprisonment for pocketing a shilling which he picked off the counter, and in 1896 Whiteley sued a clerk who had been twelve years in his employ, who was married, and was helping to support his mother, brother, and sisters, for stealing "on a sudden impulse" the sum of two shillings, which, when accused, he immediately offered to return! From 1890 onward errand-boys and delivery-men were constantly being prosecuted for withholding small sums paid them by customers. In short, the amount of petty thieving for which Whiteley felt himself called upon to put his employees in the dock was more than was good for his reputation as a manager of men.

There was one other feature of Whiteley's character, necessarily obscure in its details, which yet played an important part in the ultimate tragedy of his life. The Universal Provider, soon after his establishment in Westbourne Grove, began to acquire the name of a ladies' man. This was due not merely to his popularity with his lady customers, but also to rumours of the gay life which he led when 'off duty.' Whiteley did not always proceed at the week-end to his country home at Finchley, there to enjoy domestic and rural pursuits. On the contrary, he formed the habit of going off to visit Brighton and other places, in company with a friend named George Rayner, a financier of some prominence in the City. They were attracted to Brighton by the charms of two young ladies with whom they had become acquainted. These two girls were sisters, daughters of an ornamental plasterer, Thomas Turner, of Belvedere, in Kent. They were both very pretty, but the stock from which they had sprung was not a sound one, since their mother, grandmother, and other relations had all suffered from excessive addiction to alcohol. Emily, the younger, born in 1858, had at the age of about sixteen gone into service as nursemaid in the house of a barrister in Tavistock Square, London. Two years later she met George Rayner, who was then living in Gray's Inn, formed an attachment for him, and went to live with him in a furnished house which he provided in Stanley Road, Teddington. Of this *liaison* there soon appeared results in the shape of two boys and a girl; but, unfortunately, the paternity of the two boys was at times a matter of argument between Emily and George, since the latter repudiated responsibility for their origin. He therefore sent the elder away at an early age to be looked after elsewhere, but was persuaded to acknowledge and bring up the younger boy, whom his mother had registered in the name of Horace George Rayner at his birth in April 1879 at Teddington. This child of dubious paternity was fated, through a strange sequence of chances, to haunt the closing stages of Whiteley's life and to be the instrument of his awful end.

Emily's sister, Louisa, who was two years her elder, had been employed first in a toyshop, next as a barmaid, and afterwards as a lady clerk in a brewery in Romford. But after only a few months in this latter situation she applied for an engagement as shop assistant in Whiteley's, where she was given a job in the toy department. Like the other girl assistants, she ' lived in ' at the firm's lodging-house, and in the course of her duties she attracted her employer's attention because of her good looks. Whiteley soon commenced to pay his new employee attentions, such as taking her out driving and giving her presents. Louisa, or " Louie " as her friends and admirers called her, was evidently a girl of spirit. She had the courage to tell the Universal Provider that she thought the scarlet and gold liveries in which he dressed his coachmen and footmen too loud; and Whiteley was so impressed that he changed them, and at her suggestion substituted plain black liveries.

Sooner or later George Rayner and William Whiteley discovered that they had formed attachments to two sisters, and thereafter they frequently paid their addresses together. Apartments were taken in the New Steyne, Brighton, whither the two girls with their lovers would go off at week-ends. It was a gay life, and all went smoothly until Mrs Whiteley's suspicions began to be roused; she became convinced that her husband was unfaithful to her. According to her own account long afterwards, matters came to a head in the spring of 1881, when, in consequence of a chance remark, a quarrel broke out which resulted in Mrs Whiteley's, at the end of July, taking the step of suddenly leaving her husband's house at Finchley and going, together with her younger children and their governess, to stay at Folkestone, where her eldest boy was at school. As soon as the Universal Provider learned of his wife's departure he followed her down to Folkestone for an interview; but, according to accounts that appeared in the newspapers, Mrs Whiteley, perhaps influenced by her governess, locked herself in her bedroom and refused to see him. Whiteley had to return to town without achieving his object, and the incident hardened his heart. In August Mrs Whiteley filed a petition for judicial separation, alleging adultery and cruelty against her husband. Then followed protracted legal proceedings, first about a subsistence allowance for Mrs Whiteley, and subsequently about the custody of the children. In the course of the former Whiteley was compelled to disclose the amount of his net annual income, which he estimated at £15,000 a year. The dispute over the children centred round the choice of schools for the elder and the choice of a governess for the younger. At the end of November the courts decided in Whiteley's favour on the first point, but in Mrs Whiteley's favour on the second. The hearing of her divorce petition was due to come up before the High Court late in the summer of 1882. At the last moment Mrs Whiteley was induced by her solicitor to come to a compromise with her husband, on terms which were financially favourable to her. They agreed to live separately, Whiteley allowing his wife £2000 a year; and this separation, once accomplished, continued for the rest of their lives.

While this settlement was being reached, in order to give time for the scandal occasioned by what the newspapers called "the Great Whiteley Divorce" to subside, Whiteley moved Louisa Turner from his shop and temporarily employed her as housekeeper on his farm at Finchley. Then, when the storm was over, he quietly rented and furnished for her a house in Greville Road, Kilburn, where she lived under his protection for several years, during the course of which in 1885 she bore him a son called Cecil. The *ménage* in Kilburn had several curious features. Whiteley had taken the premises in the name of his friend Rayner, explaining that the house was intended to accommodate George Rayner and Emily Turner as well as Louisa if they chose to live there. But in fact, though both rent and rates continued to be paid in the name of Rayner, George and Emily proved only occasional visitors. Sometimes they would come to stay in Greville Road, and at other times Whiteley and Louisa would go down to Brighton to pay them a return visit. It was on one of these latter visits during 1883 or 1884 that the Universal Provider was first seen by the young boy, Horace, who was then only four or five years old. A little later Horace was taken by his mother to London to visit the great stores in Westbourne Grove. There he was noticed by Whiteley, who must have created upon his childish mind a deep impression of power and affluence. Then in due course Horace was taken by his mother on one of her visits to stay with Aunt Louisa in Greville Road. There again he used to see Whiteley frequently about the place, especially at breakfast-time. And so there gradually grew up in his mind the notion that the Universal Provider, rich, powerful, domineering as he was, must have some close connexion through his aunt with his mother and himself.

But in 1888 occurred an episode which entirely changed the current of these relationships. George

WHITELEY AND HIS TWO SONS AND DAUGHTERS
About the year 1885.
From *The Daily Mirror*

Rayner and William Whiteley fell out, and ceased to be friends—in fact, became bitter enemies. The quarrel between them was caused by Whiteley's jealousy of attentions which he believed Rayner was paying to Louisa. He referred to his former friend in terms which the latter resented so deeply as to threaten him with an action for slander. The case was actually put into solicitors' hands, and though it never came into court, the old friendship was never resumed. In May 1888 Whiteley ceased to live with Louisa Turner, though he continued to allow her £150 a year; and about the same time George Rayner separated from Emily Turner, who later married a racing man, and died at Southampton in 1898.

Meanwhile young Horace, who had been receiving his education at various schools, including a Catholic school at Rugby, parted from his mother in 1894, and went to live with George Rayner. He was now at the impressionable age of fourteen or fifteen, and beginning to become conscious of the peculiarity of his parentage and status. The circumstances which had arisen made it unlikely that his foster-father, George Rayner, would refer in his presence to either Whiteley or Emily in flattering terms. Rayner, in fact, treated the growing boy more as a companion than as a ward, and did not hesitate to express himself frankly about matters usually kept hidden from children. From time to time, when he had taken more drink than was good for him, he would suggest to the unfortunate youth that he was not really entitled to the name of Rayner at all—that his paternity was doubtful, that he ought to look for maintenance not to George Rayner, but to William Whiteley, upon whom he had a more real claim. And so in Horace's mind germinated the fatal idea that he was really an illegitimate son by Emily Turner of the Universal Provider. The shock was at first hard to endure—so much so that on one occasion, when he was sixteen, young Horace, after hearing Rayner repeat his cruel suggestion, took him at his word, ran away, and for two days tramped about the streets of London in solitude. He did not at that time make his way to Westbourne Grove or attempt to see Whiteley. But who knows what strange complex the suggestion may not have set up in him towards his alleged father—this man who, he believed, had seduced his mother and evaded, or possibly even denied, the responsibilities he owed to her child? Things forgotten, actions half remembered, would come back to life and gain a new significance in his disordered thoughts. Truly George Rayner in his drunken fit had lighted the fires of a strange revenge for the slight he fancied he had suffered; and truly William Whiteley was to reap late in life a bitter harvest from the wild oats he had sown so gaily in the heyday of his manhood!

CHAPTER V

Ordeal by Fire

NEARLY twenty years of toil had now brought Whiteley within sight of realizing the dream of his youth. In the eighteen shops which he had established in the Grove the Great Exhibition of 1851 might seem to live again. No stately Hyde Park elms, of course—only the ghosts of trees in this wood-paved Grove. No galleries, vaults, and pinnacles of glass—only a long row of windows stretching down the dusty pavement. The outside might fall short of the ideal; but inside what a stock of goods had been assembled, what a mighty profit had been distilled out of importing the cheap products of all the countries of the world! Whiteley, though in later years a churchgoer, could hardly be described as a religious man; he was the friend of Labouchere and supporter of Bradlaugh. But he had chosen for himself the title of "Universal Provider," and this curious mimicry of the Almighty showed at any rate a resolution not to be content with dreams and visions, but to insist on their translation into material substance—"building Jerusalem in England's green and pleasant land," but with himself as landlord, architect, and contractor. Well, Whiteley had achieved something, but at what a cost! He had roused bitter animosity among his fellow-tradesmen. He had defied the authority of the locality where he lived. He had imposed an iron discipline upon his servants. He had crushed and driven forth opposition within his own household. But, as a result, there was no man better known or more hated in Bayswater. To his customers he was indeed the "Universal Provider," who cared assiduously for their wants, who offered to nurse them from the cradle to the grave, who received them always with a fatherly smile and with inscrutable courtesy. But behind the scenes, outside the doors of his Paradise, round the corner—did there not lurk enemies who grudged him his prosperity, hated his methods, and cried out for his downfall? And was there not within himself another enemy, that depreciated his own achievements, pointed the contrast between his tawdry collection of shops and Paxton's inspired palace, and urged him ever on to "pull down his barns and build greater," and so narrow the gap between dream and reality?

For five years Westbourne Grove was to be haunted by the demon of fire—fire, the bane of the shopkeeper. That November day in 1876, when the Bayswater butchers burned him in effigy, had brought the smell of it under Whiteley's nose. He had watched the demonstration with a smile upon his face, but had none the less made his preparations coolly and cautiously. First he insured his buildings, both the old in Westbourne Grove and the new in Queen's Road; also the stock, whose book value had reached nearly a quarter of a million pounds. Then on every floor of his buildings at each partition wall he installed iron doors, the closing of which might stop draught and so prevent any outbreak of fire, if one occurred, from spreading. Finally he engaged two firemen, whose duty it was to patrol the place at night both inside and outside the buildings, and see that all was safe. No one now slept on the premises in Westbourne Grove; only at one end of the new Queen's Road block was the big dormitory that housed three hundred of Whiteley's young men.

At a quarter-past eleven on the evening of Thursday, November 16, 1882, a resident in Queen's Road was standing on his doorstep, taking a breath of air (the night was fine) before turning in to bed, when he heard a stranger call out as he ran past up the street, "Whiteley's is in flames—if you want to see a blaze!" Five minutes later curiosity had brought the resident out, to join a small group that stood on the pavement watching a light which they could see flickering inside a window on the second floor of No. 51 Westbourne Grove, which housed Whiteley's stock of ribbons, feathers, and artificial flowers. The stranger's message seemed mysterious; there was no blaze yet, only the beginnings of one. While they watched four persons arrived in a hurry, found a door, and disappeared into the interior of the shop. One was a policeman, two were firemen, and the fourth was Whiteley, who had just been fetched from his house in Kildare Terrace. Whiteley had been working late, as was his custom, and had not left the Westbourne Grove premises until a quarter to eleven; twenty minutes later Duke, the fireman, had discovered the fire and given the alarm. Whiteley was his usual calm self; he evidently thought that with the aid of his own firemen he could bring the blaze under control. Even when this hope vanished, and the flames a few minutes later were seen bursting through the roof, he was able, as he moved through the crowd, to reassure those who feared that some members of his staff might be trapped inside. Soon the fire-engines—thirteen worked by steam and ten by hand—arrived and began to flood the place with water, while two hundred of Whiteley's employees, fetched from the dormitory in Queen's Road, assisted the London Salvage Corps to remove whatever stock they could from the burning building. But the fire would not be put out; it spread both ways along the Grove, and involved in all six shops housing the cotton, wool, silk, and stationery departments.

At last, about two o'clock in the morning, the blaze was overcome, but not until one of the firemen had been seriously injured by the collapse of a staircase. Much alarm was caused among the private residents living in Kensington Gardens Square at the back of Whiteley's, and many of them spent the night packing and removing their household goods. But the chief victim of the disaster continued to show remarkable self-control. Though three floors of each of the six affected shops had been burned out, and their basements were flooded with water, he gave orders that the other departments were to open and carry on as usual. Next morning the public were thronging the ground floor behind the still smoking building as though nothing had happened. Meantime the proprietor himself was coolly conducting over the scene of the fire the representative of the *Bayswater Chronicle*, his bitterest public critic. They surveyed together a scene of devastation, " costly glass showcases, rocking-horses, mantles, and the incalculable miscellanea of a ' Universal Provider ' buried under heaps of blackened and sodden *débris* "; and the reporter noted that in the basement, which had once been a refreshment-room, " the ceiling and floors suggest the invasion of a high tide of the Thames." Altogether damage had been done to the extent of £42,000; but, fortunately for Whiteley, both buildings and stock were fully covered by insurance, effected mainly with the Royal Fire Office.

No one could discover the cause of the fire, the most plausible theory being that it must have originated with a gas leak. It was, however, admittedly the biggest that had yet been seen in Bayswater, and throughout the following week—especially on the Sunday—crowds of visitors came to Westbourne Grove to have a look at the ruins. The Universal Provider himself was moved to make a departure from his usual custom and insert an advertisement in the papers:

> Wm. Whiteley begs most respectfully to express his appreciation and to convey his sincere thanks to his numerous customers for their very kind and considerate expressions of sympathy and good wishes. He has pleasure to inform them that his business is now being conducted in all the several branches as formerly, and also that not one single member of his staff has been thrown out of employment.

It was a proud boast, but ill-timed—when interpreted in the light of the salvage sale that followed immediately, announced by Whiteley on a huge flag that hung over the ruins. An extraordinary scene occurred on Monday, December 11, when the sale began in foggy, unpleasant weather.

> Long before the doors opened a huge crowd of women stood close up to the windows and overflowed into the road, and for some hours the crowd was fed by newcomers, till the street was filled with a struggling mob presenting a by no means decorous appearance, the usual proportion of female shop-thieves being present. According to the complaint of several in the crowd, many women of the reputable class were sadly hustled in the unsuccessful attempt

> to enter the premises, which in course of time was declared to be full, although the announcement failed to disperse the outsiders, who stuck to their posts with the energy and persistence which the salvage shopper alone can display.

Whiteley was severely criticized for allowing only two doors of his establishment to be opened, one at No. 41 for ingress, guarded by " two distracted-looking policemen," and another for egress. Commented one lady:

> The sight of the poor, struggling women who heroically fought their way to the counter, anxious to secure bargains for their families in spite of their clothes being nearly torn off their backs—to say nothing of the intoxicated appearance their heads presented by their headgear slipping about—was truly touching.

Indeed, the scramble revealed the elements of a class war. Proletarian bargain-hunters from Notting Hill claimed the sale as their own, and resented, in rough language, the intrusion of plutocrats from Prince's Square or Lancaster Gate, who operated under pretence of buying to stock charity bazaars or aiding the district visitor.

The conjunction of fire and sale was now provoking a good deal of unfriendly comment. Thus the *Bayswater Chronicle* ominously " hoped Mr Whiteley has had his last public fire, as the mob of struggling women at the salvage sale was a sight to make men blush." The sale was not to be repeated; but the fire was. Bayswater forgot Whiteley for a moment, to enjoy its Christmas dinner in muggy, misty weather: but before daylight on Boxing Day smoke was observed to be issuing from the fifth floor of a block of buildings behind the new row of shops in Queen's Road. This block comprised Whiteley's furniture workshop, printing works, and piano-manufacturing department. A hundred and forty workmen who were employed here had left work as usual on Saturday for their Christmas holiday; the gas-engines which drove the machinery had been extinguished, and the premises subsequently patrolled at regular intervals by watchmen and firemen. Christmas Day fell on the Monday, so the buildings had been empty for over forty-eight hours when the fire broke out. Once again it spread with preternatural rapidity, and in half an hour had gained a firm hold on the dried varnished woods and gilded substances which filled the piano workshops. At seven o'clock, while twenty engines were playing upon the fire, Whiteley himself arrived on the scene, just in time to see the roof fall in and hear the heavy printing machinery crash through the upper floor with a noise like thunder. As the uncontrolled flames leaped high in the air the crowds of spectators who stood by watching were appalled to hear a series of piercing shrieks, which they guessed must proceed from some human victim trapped in the burning building. But it was only the denizens of Whiteley's menagerie, a collection of monkeys, marmosets, cockatoos, and parakeets, housed in the provision warehouse at the foot of the blazing factory. Hard by, Douglas Place was crowded with women and children who had evacuated the adjacent houses, and with seventy cart-horses brought out from Whiteley's stables for safety. It was characteristic of the *sang-froid* of their owner that as soon as he saw them he gave orders that they should be put back again into their stables.

News of the conflagration spread far and wide, and

holidaymakers who had been spending Christmas night in jollification hastened up in droves to enjoy the spectacle. A good deal of sarcasm was openly expressed at Whiteley's expense. Thus the *Bayswater Chronicle* hardly troubled to conceal its jeers:

> In Bayswater Boxing Day was celebrated with an illumination gratuitously provided by Mr Whiteley. The fire was a public boon, judging from the animated and gala appearance of the traffic. People seemed perfectly thankful to have something to visit and gaze at on so black a day. The sudden animation which marked the streets was noticeable; indeed, it is remarkable how exhilarating a good conflagration always is. As there was no skating on Boxing Day, and Mr Whiteley's fire was extinguished somewhat too early for the general holiday-maker, there was a decided flagging in the day's programme until the theatres opened for the pantomime. As a last resource many betook themselves in a fit of despair to the public swimming baths at Queen's Road.

The more tender-hearted members of the public visited the menagerie, which was a new feature of Whiteley's, only opened in 1882, to make sure that their pet animals and birds had not suffered in the fire.

Shortly after midday the hoses ceased to play upon the smoking ruins, and Whiteley, accompanied, as before, by a representative of the *Bayswater Chronicle*, began a tour of inspection. On the first floor lay twisted printing machinery, above it sodden furniture. On the fourth floor

> the slates of the fallen roof and bricks of the crumbling walls lay mingled with charred pianos and the costliest drawing-room and boudoir furniture and knickknacks. Glistening in the charred *débris* were fragments of costly silver mirrors, shining like crystals embedded in the blackened mass; fragments of richly gilded Louis Quatorze

furniture and Marie-Antoinette writing-tables lay mingled with broken gas-engines and fly-wheels and engine straps and gear.

A heap of blackened powder was all that remained of over a hundred pianos that had dropped through the top floor and been consumed below. Much of the destroyed furniture consisted of articles sent by customers to the workshops for repair—for which the Universal Provider had to accept responsibility. Fortunately for him, however, the damage both to buildings and to contents was covered by insurance. For a day or two wild rumours ran round the Grove: the fires were more than an accident—Whiteley was involved; he was about to be arrested. But time put an end to these *canards*. The origin of the second fire remained even more wrapped in mystery than the origin of the first. The insurance companies paid up, but refused to renew their policies, except at an increase in rates of premium. Even Whiteley's neighbours had to pay more, because their shops were near his.

While the burned buildings were being re-erected Whiteley had his hands full again in carrying a stage farther his struggle with the Paddington Vestry. That body, indeed, was showing some signs of war-weariness. At the beginning of February 1883 was published the voluminous correspondence which had been carried on for over a year between the Vestry and the Local Government Board concerning the Board's refusal to sanction the loan of £3000 required to enable the Baths Commissioners to build their wall against Whiteley's new Queen's Road dormitory. This correspondence, when printed, occupied 143 pages, and had involved both parties in considerable expense. It yielded, however, one satisfaction to the Vestry. In the closing stages of the correspondence the Local Government Board gave way about the wall, and on March 6 James Flood was able to announce in the Vestry meeting that they had permission to borrow £2000 to build the screen wall and £874 to underpin the Baths against Whiteley's lowered foundations. But the victory was Pyrrhic. The Vestry elections were approaching, and Flood was sensible that his long domination was threatened by a revolt of part of the ratepayers. For nearly ten years the policy of the Paddington Vestry had been controlled by a group of tradesmen who, while they were gratifying their animosity against the Universal Provider, were meeting the increased local expenditure by raising the assessments on the houses of the Bayswater aristocracy proportionately higher than the assessment on their own shops and offices. Now these richer residents were also Whiteley's customers, and so his cause was theirs. Flood and his group of tradesmen attacked Whiteley, and the expense involved was laid upon his best customers. It was natural that the two aggrieved parties should draw together in a common opposition.

Becoming aware of this danger, Flood moderated his attitude to Whiteley. At the meeting on March 6 he refrained from pressing on with his wall-building scheme, but proposed instead a postponement to allow time for opening negotiations with Whiteley. A month later the Vestry appointed a committee of three to meet their enemy and discuss their differences, with full power to settle. At the same meeting Flood was defeated in his attempt to secure re-election on the Assessment Committee of the Vestry; while early in

May he retained by a bare five votes his place as Chairman of the Baths Commissioners. These evident signs of unpopularity, combined with failing health, induced him to announce his withdrawal from public life. But though Flood was not a candidate in the Vestry elections that May, his place as leader of the anti-Whiteley faction was taken by William Owen, who was firmly established as the Universal Provider's biggest rival in Westbourne Grove. For his part Whiteley strained every nerve to alter the composition of the Vestry in his favour, especially in Ward 1, which included the Grove. His influence was exerted "both financially and personally," and every householder in the Ward was circularized three times. But the result on May 22 was disappointing: the five Whiteley candidates just failed to beat their opponents, and two tradesmen, Record and Owen, were among the victors. Nevertheless the contest had been salutary in one respect: the anti-Whiteley party did not care to pursue the vendetta, and the negotiations previously initiated were carried on during the rest of the year.

For Whiteley too was not in a position to fight to a finish. His time and energy were fully occupied in yet another of those pieces of tangled litigation into which he was always being drawn. He had become embroiled with a Bishopsgate brush-manufacturer and dealer named Rooney, who sued him for two sums of £811 and £2600 said to be due for goods which he had supplied to Whiteley. The latter disputed liability for the debt on the ground that Rooney was implicated in a scheme for bribing his (Whiteley's) buyers. The case had a long history, dating back to the prosecution of the five young men who were convicted in 1880 of conspiracy to defraud the Universal Provider. One of the five who received sentences of imprisonment was a brother of Rooney. In the next year, 1881, Rooney's solicitor was instrumental in securing the disgrace of Whiteley's solicitor, C. M. Roche, when the latter was struck off the roll of solicitors for two years. Now Whiteley alleged that Rooney was bribing his buyers by paying them a commission on the brushes that he sold them—a charge which Rooney repudiated on the ground that such commissions were a usual trade custom. The merits of the case were of less public interest than the fact that it came before the Divisional Court no less than sixteen times, and before the Appeal Court twice, before being sent finally to arbitration by a judge's order in June 1883. In all 140 summonses were taken out, and the proceedings were computed to have cost nearly £10,000.

Whiteley's third fire broke out on the afternoon of Saturday, April 26, 1884. This affected the warehouses which had been erected five years previously at such great cost in Queen's Road on the north side of the Baths. It was to block the Peeping Toms from the windows of these buildings that the Baths Commissioners had erected their first wall. As on the previous occasions, there was no holding the blaze once it had been discovered. The fire started in the carpet department of No. 147, and spread until the whole row of five shops, Nos. 147 to 155 Queen's Road, was burned out. These shops contained the furniture, furnishing drapery, linen, blankets, trunks and cases, china and glass departments. The provision departments and the livestock in the zoological department escaped untouched. The fire burned on late into the night, and

" the glow in the clouds was distinctly seen by countrymen coming with their haycarts from Sudbury and Harrow." Large crowds of sightseers were conveyed to the scene in omnibuses whose proprietors displayed placards bearing the words " To Whiteley's Fire." At the height of the conflagration the Mansard roof with its tower and flag fell in, and a loud explosion followed as the gas-pipes burst; it took an hour to cut off the supply at the mains.

Next day traffic in the neighbourhood was completely disorganized. Wooden barriers had to be erected across Queen's Road, and " a great unwashed and evil-looking crowd from the East End of London thronged the streets, apparently enjoying the sight." The whole neighbourhood was invaded by street-singers, performing Zulus, and other itinerants; indeed, " the residents of Kensington Gardens Square probably saw more of the masses of London in one brief hour than during the whole of their previous existence." The firemen continued to play their hoses on the smoking ruins, and some of the spectators compared the scene with the broken front of the Tuileries in the days of the Paris Commune. Meanwhile business at the great emporium was carried on as usual; and by half-past eleven that morning "the dainty young ladies in their white caps and black dresses were displaying their goods with remarkable and impetuous ability, notwithstanding the chatter around them." Their employer set them an example by the unruffled equanimity with which he received the *Bayswater Chronicle* reporter, and assessed for his benefit the extent of the calamity which had befallen him. The Universal Provider, indeed, presented an odd appearance, with his coat collar turned up to his eyes, his face blackened by smoke, his hands thick with dirt, and the spray from the fire-hose standing like dewdrops on his ample whiskers. " Well," he began with his usual smile,

> the time of year is certainly most unfortunate for a fire. It happens, you see, just in time to spoil the three months' season which is just beginning, and then most likely there will be six months or more spent in rebuilding. However, there is business to be done to-day. The provision shop will be opened as usual, and I must look in and speak about it—and then the men will want their dinners as usual, and these things must be seen to, you know. . . . Yes, the fire broke out in the carpet-planning and -cutting department. Whatever is the cause of the outbreak I cannot tell you. I have no theory whatever. It dazes me, the whole thing; it is a poser to me, and a terrible, terrible loss. . . . Why, the place is the apple of my eye, built on my own freehold of the very best materials—no expense spared, I can tell you! No jerry materials. All my experience was brought to bear in the planning and devising, too. It was to be a monument for myself, for my sons and my sons' sons after them. It is really cruel. I reckon the loss of property—that is, the buildings—to be £100,000 solid. Then the stores consumed—stuffs and linens, the furnishing department, the pianos, carpets, china, glass, the workshops—all are gone, £100,000 worth of them. Then I reckon another £50,000 for the fixtures. Then my pantechnicon is gone; that is where my clients were allowed to store all kinds of private goods, and that is all burned. . . . We shall begin to build as soon as possible again, of course. I am no sooner down than up again.

Whiteley, as was natural, somewhat exaggerated the value of the damage done, which amounted in the end to about £123,000. Of this about half (£62,000) was recovered from the Royal, Mutual, Equitable, and other insurance companies. But there remained the formidable sum of £61,000 to be accounted for in the balance-sheet at the end of February 1885. Nor did the damage done by the fire mark the limit of the loss sustained by the firm. Business was severely affected, and at the same time the burned shops had to be rebuilt and restocked. The year's trading showed a net loss of £105,000; the value of the item "Stock" in the balance-sheet was reduced from £262,000 to £164,000; while the item "Sundry Creditors," which included bank deposits, rose by £10,000 to £213,000. Thus Whiteley overcame the effects of the disaster not only by sacrificing several years' income, but by borrowing more from his customers and omitting to replace much of the stock which had been burned.

A by-product of the conflagration was the destruction of the rival walls which had been built by Whiteley and the Paddington Baths Commission during their feud five years earlier. The fire had brought down Whiteley's wall, with its ninety-five orifices, and severely warped the Commissioners' wall, which had to be condemned as unsafe. Then, only five days after the fire, the latter suddenly toppled over and buried a party of workmen who had been engaged by the Royal Insurance Company to commence pulling it down. Eleven men were injured, and two of them subsequently brought actions against Whiteley, one of whom was awarded twenty pounds compensation. For the rest of that year the Universal Provider found his trade much hampered by the partial closing of Queen's Road to traffic, to allow of the rebuilding of his burned premises. In his hurry to reopen he placed his builder under contract to complete his task by December 31 or pay fifty pounds penalty for every day's delay. But though he prohibited the use of matchboarding throughout, and arranged to have all floors made of concrete, he found the insurance companies shy of renewing his fire policies. In March 1884 the companies, ostensibly because of Fenian dynamite outrages in the City, reduced their big risks by 75 per cent., and this included a refusal to take further responsibility for Whiteley's stock and fittings or any of the buildings which belonged to him. One consequence of this serious setback was to induce in Whiteley a more conciliatory attitude towards his old foes on the Paddington Vestry. The long struggle, which had continued intermittently for nearly ten years, was brought to a close at the beginning of April, when the negotiating committee announced that a compromise had been reached. By it the Baths Commissioners renounced their project for building a gigantic wall *vis-à-vis* Whiteley's windows in Queen's Road, in consideration of the latter's paying an annual sum of twenty pounds for light and air. He was also to concede the existence of a public right of way in Douglas Place, and to pay £300 as compensation for obstruction. With regard to the drainage controversy, Whiteley was successful in avoiding the order to lower his pipes to the level desired by the Vestry—the drawback being, as the *Bayswater Chronicle* noted, the risk that " at times the main sewage of the parish will rise above Whiteley's pipes and imprison the house sewage, possibly for days together."

Another sign of the anxiety which his fire risks and losses were causing the Universal Provider was a fresh outburst of enterprise on his part, designed to attract new custom. At the end of June he found a successor to Cetewayo in the Maori King Tawhiao, who had come from New Zealand to visit London. Tawhiao drew crowds of sightseers to gape at his blue tattooed visage as he inspected the shops, took luncheon in Whiteley's refreshment-room, and was escorted off the premises by the Universal Provider himself. A fortnight later a fresh sensation was caused by the installation of a huge circular electric fan in the basement of the Queen's Road shop. In half an hour this halved a temperature which had previously measured 115 degrees Fahrenheit!

But the most substantial token that Whiteley could give of his determination to rise above all disasters was the posting at the end of the year to his customers of his gigantic *Illustrated Catalogue and General Price List for* 1885. This volume, nearly as bulky as a family Bible, set forth in 1293 pages, with plans and illustrations, the copious glories of the mighty emporium. The list of contents alone filled twenty-five pages, and suggested that the Universal Provider had indeed achieved his ambition of translating the Great Exhibition into a great bazaar. In an elaborate and rather unctuous preface he expounded his business methods, begging leave

> most respectfully to point out that the goods are quoted at a very low rate of profit for ready money exclusively, without discount, and that in the calculation of price no margin is allowed for bad debts, advertising, interest on overdue accounts, and other contingencies incidental to every trade. The system of business being both to buy and sell for ready money, he is enabled to make his purchases on the most favourable terms and in the best and cheapest market in the world; and as it is a principle with him not

to allow himself to be undersold, he feels the utmost confidence in asserting that his goods will be found to be of the best value obtainable. This system he originally adopted, and has always adhered to; and the rapid and unprecedented development of this Establishment is a proof how much it is appreciated by the public. The unbounded resources of this Establishment, and the extraordinary advantages it offers to customers both at home and abroad are now widely known. It is sufficient therefore to say that in no other Establishment in the world can goods of every description be purchased with such great economy of money, time, trouble, and fatigue; to this it owes its unequalled success, which is believed to be without parallel in the history of commerce.

The boast was a proud one; but the succeeding pages of the catalogue went far to justify it. From its almost bewildering mass of detail space permits only the quotation of a few outstanding typical or peculiar features. The prices were certainly moderate. A lady's riding-habit could be bought for 70*s.*, *a* tennis racquet for 12*s.* 9*d.*, a gentleman's felt hat for 3*s.* 6*d.*, silk stockings for 6*s.* 11*d.* (white) or 7*s.* 11*d.* (black), corsets for 4*s.* 9*d.*, and crinolines for 10*s.* A complete funeral could be furnished for £5 10*s.* In millinery, " special arrangements having been concluded with the most celebrated Parisian *modistes* for an early supply of novelties, the models of the season are shown and copies may be had as soon as they are produced in Paris." Oriental embroideries from all parts of the Turkish Empire and Persia were offered at prices from a shilling and a halfpenny upward. A large section of the catalogue was devoted to ladies' fancy work, including all those delights of the Victorian boudoir—needlework, cross-stitch, traced cloth-work, crewel

FASHIONS, 1885

Plate from William Whiteley's catalogue of 1885

and outline-work, leather-work, braiding, cushion-trimming, knitting, crochet, etc. Forty pages were occupied with books, which, according to the system of selling then in force, were offered at 25 per cent. discount off published price. You could get the *Athenæum* bound up at the modest rate of 2*s.* 7*d.* per volume. In the stationery and printing section a novelty was offered, to order only at £18, in the form of Remington's Perfected Typewriter, quaintly described as

> a machine to supersede the pen for manuscript-writing. . . . It is especially demanded by lawyers, compositors, editors, authors, and journalists, and all who write for the Press. No solicitor can afford to be without one of these machines. . . . Clergymen, especially those who prepare their sermons in full, will experience all the advantages of having a clearly printed sermon to read at less than half the expense in time and labour of a written one.

The advertisement went on to guarantee the operator against soiling his fingers or clothing, and re-assured him against "fear of pen paralysis, loss of sight, or curvature of the spine from using the machine."

The hairdressing department sought to attract gentlemen by providing them with a daily shave on the basis of a yearly subscription of £1, and ladies by the offer of "Whiteley's invisible scalpette for thin and bald places, made to any size in curled and waved toupees in all colours." The drug department listed an enormous selection of patent medicines, ranging from Blair's Gout Pills, Cockle's Anti-bilious Pills, Crosthwaite's Pain-killer, Dredge's Heal-all, Gabriel's Sedadent, Parr's Life Pills, and Widow Welsh's Pills to Woodcock's Wind Pills and boxes of Beetle-paste. Rather surprisingly, in view of the prejudices of the age, the list included one or two contraceptives.

One of the biggest sections was that devoted to furniture. Whiteley's estimate for furnishing completely an eight-roomed house throws an interesting light on the domestic economy of the eighties. It was distributed as follows:

	£.	s.	d.
Hall and stairs	5	17	6
Dining-room	51	7	6
Breakfast-room	13	11	7
Drawing-room	62	1	9
Best bedroom	52	3	8
Spare bedroom	28	12	9½
Bachelor's room	17	10	10
Servant's bedroom	7	17	2½
Kitchen	7	6	0
Total of furniture	£236	8	10½
China and glass	9	3	8
Electroplate and cutlery	12	19	5½
Ironmongery	7	9	7½
Brushes and turnery	2	9	3½
Grand total	£268	10	9½

This sum (which, it will be noted, was wrongly added up) allowed in the dining-room for a mahogany suite, including a striking clock, and a sideboard with glass back and cellaret; in the drawing-room for a walnut suite, with a fourteen-day ormolu clock, a what-not, and two pairs of chenille curtains; in the best bedroom for a solid ash suite, a 5 ft. 6 in. feather bolster with two pillows, and foot- and hip-bath; in the spare bedroom for a straw palliasse, a wool mattress, a fireguard, and a hip-bath; and in the bachelor's room for a sponge-bath. The palliasses and mattresses were carefully graded in width, 4 ft. 6 ins. in the spare room, 3 ft. 6 ins. in the bachelor's room, and 2 ft. 6 ins. in the servant's room. Whiteley also catered for soldiers, to whom he offered an expensive camping kit, including

LUXURIOSUM
From the catalogue of 1885

" the only bedstead that is made capable of sustaining an amount of weight when standing on an uneven surface."

In the china section particular attention is called to the stock of

> ' sardine ' boxes, egg-stands, Carlton sets, metal-covered jugs, *tête-à-tête* services, butter-dishes, etc. The new Whiteley Lawn-tennis tables with revolving china tops, and with cups and saucers to match, are greatly appreciated. Orders taken for these will be executed in turn, as it has been found impossible to obtain them fast enough to meet the demand.

There were many glass ornaments of hideous design, including " a sexangular flowerpot on a plate-glass-mirror plateau, mounted upon best maroon velvet plinths," which was recommended for the centre of dining-tables.

The ironmongery department included many utensils

SEXANGULAR FLOWERPOT
From the catalogue of 1885

that have since gone out of fashion, such as 'jack-screens,' spittoons, travelling baths, knife-cleaners—as well as some that were just coming into fashion, such as gas-cookers. A large section was given over to engines and implements of all kinds, especially agricultural. The hire department offered to furnish dinners, wedding breakfasts, ball suppers, evening parties, *fêtes,* and so forth, and to send goods of the best quality to any part of the United Kingdom. Besides the ordinary marquees, tents, and bazaar stalls the department lent portable theatres and scenery, dresses, bands, stage managers, rockwork grottoes, magic

TEMPORARY BALLROOM OR PAVILION
From the catalogue of 1885

lanterns, pianos, flags, and a variety of entertainments by conjurers, ventriloquists, marionettes, nigger minstrels, and performing animals. A marionette pantomime entitled *Harlequin Father Christmas*—"the whole invented and produced expressly for William Whiteley"—could be hired for four guineas, and *The Yellow Dwarf: a New and Original Punchinello Burlesque Extravaganza,* for three guineas. The catering department offered to contract to feed Cinderella balls, laying-foundation-stone parties, water, political, or railway parties, and regimental dinners.

Then followed the provisions, flower, and vegetable sections, the banking, theatre, and travel agencies, a large sanitary section (including the offer of a substitute for stained glass), and an electric department. The great catalogue ended at last with a sporting section, a lengthy list of music publications, and sixty pages of manufacturers' advertisements, whose insertion testified to the large circulation which the volume expected to achieve. One of the most impressive features of the catalogue was the description of the delivery facilities. Whiteley's carts and vans delivered three times every day anywhere in town, daily in the suburbs (which included such distant spots as Caterham, Chingford, Chislehurst, Gerrards Cross, Harrow, Reigate, and Stoke Poges), thrice weekly in the northern and eastern outskirts, and twice weekly in the southern outskirts of London. Whiteley's was one of the first shops to install a telephone; and it was estimated that more than seven hundred omnibuses passed its doors every day, bringing shoppers to Westbourne Grove from all parts of the Metropolis.

A GARDEN UMBRELLA
From the catalogue of 1885

The issue of the great catalogue of 1885 seemed like a reaffirmation of the Universal Provider's faith in himself. His barns had been burned, but they were overflowing with goods for dispensing to the world as before. Fate, however, was ready to respond to his challenge. Little more than a year had passed since the conflagration in Queen's Road, when for the fourth time the fire-fiend raised his hand—this time in Westbourne Grove again. The old shops that had been burned down in the fire of 1882 (the first of all) had been replaced by a row of taller and handsomer buildings that stretched without a break from No. 31 to No. 55, and then jumped a gap to No. 61. These shops stood five stories high. The basements were used as warehouses, the ground floors as shops, the first floors as showrooms, and the upper floors as workrooms. In the centre of the row hung an enormous clock, which served as a rendezvous for Whiteley's customers. All the shops had recently been equipped with electric light, and there were three private hydrants indoors to ensure a good flow of water in case of need.

At this period it was Whiteley's custom to sleep out of town during the hot part of the summer season. From June to August he used to drive out in the evening to his Manor Farm at Finchley, and drive back to work in the morning. Early on the morning of Wednesday, June 17, he was awakened by a messenger who summoned him post-haste to Bayswater, which he reached soon after eight. For more than two hours a fierce fire had been raging in Westbourne Grove, in the face of the combined efforts of 24 fire-engines and 119 men. The fire was first noticed by a policeman at about ten minutes to six at No. 41, which housed the millinery and silk departments. Soon it had extended in both directions, involving every shop between No. 33 and No. 45. Four were completely burned down, including the counting-house, banking office, ticket agencies, haberdashery, hosiery, and fur departments. The books and records in the counting-house were thrown out of the windows and removed to safety, and though the fire attacked the glass bridge across Douglas Place, which connected the Westbourne Grove premises with the Queen's Road premises, it was prevented from crossing the gap, and eventually brought under control at about half-past nine. In the midst of the conflagration an odd sight was presented by a group of half-clad girls who ran out of the workpeople's entrance at No. 43 with wraps hurriedly thrown over their heads and clothing in their hands. They fled back to the dormitories in Hatherley Grove, there to take refuge and finish their interrupted toilet.

While twenty fire-engines continued to pump water on the smoking ruins the uninjured shops were opened, and customers began to be diligently served as though nothing were amiss. Whiteley himself viewed the devastation with his characteristic coolness, and replied to the eager questions of the newspaper reporter: "How did the fire originate? Well, I will tell you," he began. "We have a fireman inside in the premises and another outside all night, and every kind of precaution is taken. The men are trained firemen, recommended by Captain Shaw for their trustworthiness. This morning at half-past five the inside fireman was on the first floor of No. 41, when he thought he saw some smoke, and came down into the shop. He at once saw that one of the wrappers that cover the goods in the fixtures against the wall was on fire. It spread both right and left with alarming rapidity, so he rushed to one of the hydrants, to which hose and nozzles are always attached, and turned on the water, and began to play on the fire. . . . The iron doors on the premises did good service, and assisted very materially in keeping the fire within its ultimate bounds. But at the outset nothing could check it, as the flames burst through the walls."

"And can you not get at the cause any nearer than that?" asked the reporter.

"No, I am afraid not. At least, that has been my experience in the previous fires. I was in business for twenty years, and never claimed a penny from the insurance offices, except for some plate-glass. Then we had a fire rather more than two years ago. Although I spent no end of money in seeking to trace the origin, I failed. I got the place rebuilt, and then at Christmas 1883 [*sic*] there was a fire in the factory early on Monday morning, though it had remained perfectly safe from the time that the workmen left on Saturday afternoon. Next we had a big fire in the Queen's Road premises on the 27th April last year; and again it was impossible to discover the cause. There is no business-man who takes greater precautions. One hardly likes to think that there may be motives of business jealousy at the bottom of it."

Believing that there was evidence of incendiarism, and that the stock in the fired premises must have been primed with some combustible in more places than one, Whiteley put the matter into the hands of Scotland Yard. As his buyers agreed in suspecting a particular individual as the cause of the trouble, Whiteley offered a reward of £1000 for any information which might lead to the apprehension and conviction of the criminal; but no proof was ever forthcoming. For many months after the fire the nerves of the staff in his shops were on edge through fear of a further outbreak; and early in July one of Whiteley's girls gave an alarm which brought out all the fire-engines in the locality, because she saw through the window smoke which turned out to have come from the chimney of the Paddington Baths; while only a week later the wool department was found to be on fire, apparently through spontaneous combustion (!), but without serious consequences. Towards the end of the year the police had to take action to suppress a nuisance among local news vendors, who persisted in making night hideous in the quiet streets of Bayswater and scaring the inhabitants by shouting, "Orful discovery at Mr Whiteley's!" in order to sell their papers.

The four shops which had been burned down were each worth between two and three thousand pounds; and the total loss incurred in this fire amounted to £74,000, little of which could be recovered through insurance. Whiteley lost no time in beginning to rebuild; the work was actually completed by August 22, and the new premises opened for business on September 1, 1885. But his summer sales were severely handicapped by the effects of the fire; and though his accounts at the end of February 1886 showed a profit on the year's trading of £50,000, there was a net deficit for the year of over £20,000. The amount owed to his creditors (which included bank deposits) rose to £284,000, and he was compelled to have recourse to his bankers for a temporary loan of £25,000.

The sole consolation that the Universal Provider could derive from his ill-luck was the knowledge that at long last the tide of his unpopularity was turning. Any such suspicion as that entertained in some quarters after his first fire, that it might have suited his interests to lose stock, had been long ago dissipated. For Whiteley now no longer enjoyed protection for his property by insurance—indeed, the epidemic of fires was seriously affecting the whole neighbourhood. Residents and tradesmen had had their insurance rates raised; lodging-house keepers were becoming nervous; the value of property was being adversely affected. Accordingly, when it became known immediately after the fire that Princess Alexandra had sent a personal message of sympathy to the Universal Provider, the tradesmen of Westbourne Grove took action to show that they no longer regarded him as an upstart and an enemy. They met together and presented him with a signed address expressing their sincere and heartfelt condolence with him, and proposing to offer an additional reward of £500 for the detection of the incendiary. Whiteley was certainly pleased with this change of feeling towards him, and returned a cordial reply, though at the same time he felt bound to decline their offer.

It was, indeed, the bigger tradesmen of the neighbourhood, such as William Owen (whose shops had increased from one to seventeen in thirteen years), who took the lead in showing him friendliness. Yet evidently jealousy lingered in the background. Thus in January 1886 a Sheffield cutler sought to create prejudice against Whiteley by purchasing at his shop a pair of folding scissors for 10½*d.*, which, being far below the Sheffield price of 1*s.* 6*d.*, indicated that Whiteley was importing them from Germany. And a few months later the opening of his new photographic studio—which he boasted to be " the best in the world "—induced some enemy to denounce him to the Chemists' Trade Association, which successfully prosecuted him for selling an ounce of potassium cyanide for intensifying photographs without being a registered chemist.

These, however, were exceptions to the general rise of his prestige. In October 1886 his former enemy James Flood died, and with him were extinguished the last sparks of animosity between Whiteley and the Paddington Vestry. More significant still was the changed attitude of the local Press. Whiteley did not break his lifelong rule of refusing to buy space in the advertisement pages of any newspaper, but he conciliated both his fellow-tradesmen and the *Bayswater Chronicle* by co-operating with the former in procuring the publication in the latter of a series of original 'letters' passing between two fashionable ladies, styled "Claribel" and "Evelyn," who skilfully mixed local gossip with suitable 'puffs' for the wares of Westbourne Grove shops, including his own. Henceforth the *Chronicle* dropped its former critical and hostile tone, and printed little except what was favourable to the Universal Provider. A good impression was also created by his return to permanent residence in Bayswater. The house in Kildare Terrace had long been too small for Whiteley and his children, but it was none the less a striking reaffirmation of his faith in himself when in the autumn of 1885 he purchased for his own use No. 31 Porchester Terrace, which ranked with the larger mansions of Bayswater. This purchase, at a cost of £8000, together with his lavish expenditure upon its furnishing, greatly impressed not only his own staff, but his fellow-tradesmen and neighbours. In spite of his fire losses the Universal Provider had evidently money enough to spare for luxuries. At the house in Porchester Terrace Whiteley installed his four children under the care of a highly respectable and competent housekeeper, and from its doors he could be seen to emerge every morning punctually a few minutes before ten o'clock, arrayed in his frock-coat and top-hat, to step across the short distance which separated his own portico from the entrance to his emporium. Inside the shops his assistants waited behind their counters with some trepidation, for their employer was not only an autocrat, but punctilious in the extreme in his insistence upon tidiness and order. As he strode through the departments on his way to his own sanctum he would cast his gaze from one counter to another, and sometimes suddenly sweep off on to the floor with his umbrella any misplaced object or unsatisfactory display of goods. There were enemies still to paint an unflattering portrait of his personality. A correspondent in the *Daily Chronicle* wrote of him:

> You can see him from the outside of the bus as it slows up for the shopping ladies to alight, diffusing an atmosphere of subdued and grateful welcome among the arrivals, patting the heads of children and bowing to right and left quite in the grand forgotten style. No verger showing the Dean's lady to her stall has a more adequate manner, a finer blend of reverent blandness and gentle authority. His black frock-coat, his expressive hands always indicating even in repose welcome, expectation, gratitude, or farewell, his air of respectful friendliness, constituting a pleasing personality and lending a tone of distinction and benevolence to the whole establishment.

But

> the young ladies and gentlemen of the house declared that he has an abominable temper, and that he could lay aside his purring ways and become a regular drill-sergeant in a flash.

They tell you

> when we are unwrapping the goods and getting our stock in order for the day he just stands there and explodes—goes off into a crackle of temper by the hour. "Now then, Miss L., take care of what you are doing! You shall be instantly dismissed, miss, if I see any more of those remnants lying about!" "And, Mr D., what do you mean by putting that stuff in the window?" And so he would go on, storming, browbeating, threatening fines, reports, dismissals, till the customers began to come in, and it was time to take up the post by the door with the obsequious smile and the chilly-looking hands softly polishing one another.

During 1886 Whiteley made steady strides towards repairing the havoc caused by his previous fires, and his accounts at the end of the year (up to February 28, 1887) showed the satisfactory net profit of £75,000, the highest figure he had yet attained. Little occurred to disturb peaceful trading in Westbourne Grove—not even the ugly riots among the unemployed, which the prolonged trade depression brought to a head in February. All round Trafalgar Square shops were wrecked and plundered, and as the tide of lawlessness spread to the southern confines of Paddington cautionary telegrams began to reach Whiteley, forecasting the advance of the mob to Westbourne Grove. On the 9th and 10th of the month business was almost at a standstill. Most of the shops closed early, and the streets were deserted, save for gangs of men singing dolefully in chorus and asking for alms. Whiteley made his own preparations for dealing with the rioters if they appeared. It was said that he had laid in a stock of arms, and was prepared to issue them to his young men for self-defence. But the emergency passed, and the rioters never reached Bayswater.

That autumn and winter the ugly scenes were repeated, but soon the gloom began to be dissipated by the prospects of the approaching Jubilee of Queen Victoria in 1887. No such opportunity for public display had presented itself since the marriage of Prince Edward and Princess Alexandra a quarter of a century previously, before Westbourne Grove had emerged into fame or Whiteley had opened his first shop. He resolved that both the Grove and Queen's Road should do honour adequately to the occasion. In June 1887 he who had rigidly held aloof hitherto from local charities pleasurably surprised the neighbourhood by agreeing to co-operate in a public appeal through the churches and chapels for the provision of an entertainment on Jubilee Day for the aged deserving poor and the children of the parish. He subscribed ten guineas, and took a seat on the General Committee which organized the function. This interest in the welfare of the aged poor was a germ of the mighty idea which his will translated into a reality after his death.

Jubilee Day came at last, and gaping crowds admired the decorations which adorned the whole of Whiteley's twenty-seven shops from the roof down to the ground all along Westbourne Grove and Queen's Road. The handsome central mansard tower, "so characteristic of Parisian architecture," which sprouted upward from the Queen's Road block, was made the centre from which the whole scheme of decorations radiated. On its summit was erected a ship's mast with halyards and rigging bearing the Royal Standard and winged with pennons. Four windows on the second floor of the tower just above the clock were covered with a device representing the insignia of the Royal Family, surrounded with appropriate Shakespearean mottoes; and on the outskirts were similar devices for the colonies and dependencies, Wales, Ireland, and Scotland. Above all, the crowds admired a double festoon of drapery composed of red, white, and blue cloth, intertwined and looped with white stars, running horizontally along the whole length of the shop-fronts. But Whiteley's was beautiful only by day; for, unlike his neighbours, the Universal Provider refused to illuminate at night, no doubt through the fear of another outbreak of fire.

Hardly were the Jubilee festivities concluded with a ceremonial visit to Paddington paid by the Duke of Cambridge than the usual summer sale was launched with more than the usual animation. So July passed peaceably and profitably, and at its conclusion the holiday season opened, and Whiteley prepared to take his two boys, Frank and William, on their first trip to the Continent. They were to be away for three weeks. "I thought," he said, "the time had come for them to stretch their wings a little." On Saturday, August 7, therefore, he crossed the Channel with his boys to Ostend, where they spent the night at the Hôtel Fontaine, then rose early on Sunday morning for a walk in the gardens and sat down to morning coffee. Suddenly the British Consul at Ostend entered the lobby of the hotel with a telegram in his hand. Directed to Whiteley, he soon put the latter in possession of the appalling news that his departure from Bayswater had been the signal for another and greater conflagration among his shops.

Whiteley's own words show how he took the blow:

Naturally I was astounded, though not overpowered, by the intelligence. I did not lose my head. I asked my informant the quickest route to London; I paid my bill, ordered a cab, got the luggage together, and we made our way with

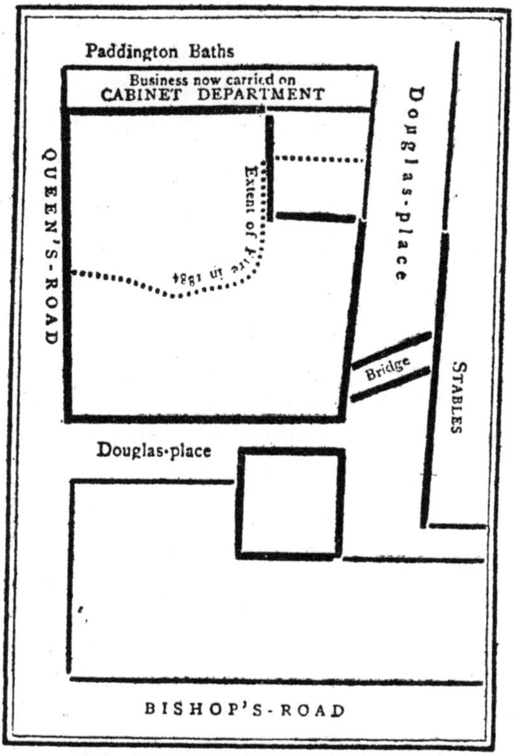

DIAGRAM SHOWING EXTENT OF THE FIRES OF 1884 AND 1887
From *The Pall Mall Budget,* August 11, 1887

all possible speed to the quay, where we were just in time to catch the vessel. So great was the haste with which we left that we were driven to the waterside by the hotel porter.

The fire-fiend had struck at the heart of the very buildings which had lately been the scene of the Jubilee glory. The block of buildings which extended from No. 147 to No. 159 Queen's Road, and which abutted upon Douglas Place, had only a few years previously been handsomely erected in York stone with strong iron girders. The buildings stood five or six stories high, and had hydrants fitted upon every floor, with iron doors between the various blocks. Firemen patrolled the premises day and night, and one of Whiteley's strictest rules was that at night the hoses should be attached to the hydrants with the branches screwed up and the deliveries laid out ready for immediate use.

All hands had left the premises at the usual hour on Saturday afternoon, August 6, after which the fireman on duty had gone over the buildings and found that everything was in order. But soon after seven o'clock a slight smell of burning attracted his attention to the Douglas Place end of the premises, which was used for manufacturing rather than retailing purposes. This place was particularly vulnerable, inasmuch as in its basement were stored great quantities of oils and drugs of every description. A brief examination showed that an outbreak of fire was raging on the second floor of this end of the building. At once the fireman turned on one of the hydrants and poured water on to the floor; but already the outbreak had got too far to be easily checked. Thick, suffocating smoke rose up in clouds and rolled along the building, while flickering bursts of flame told of a still more serious condition of affairs. At once the aid of the Metropolitan Fire Brigade was sought.

> The next quarter of an hour in the history of the progress of the fire was probably the most exciting that the oldest fireman had ever witnessed.

The Hermitage Street manual was first upon the scene, and found smoke and flames already issuing from

THE FIRE AT WHITELEY'S, SEEN FROM WEST HAMPSTEAD
From *The Illustrated London News*, August 13, 1887

half a dozen windows in the building. Determined efforts were made to check the fire at this stage.

> The first batches of firemen ran up the central staircase in Douglas Place with four lines of hose, and essayed to meet the fire face to face, pouring incessant streams of water on to the flames. The men, however, were slowly and surely beaten back. The iron doors were red hot. The whole five floors of the building were ablaze, and although the flames were kept for a little while in check upon the floor where the men were directing the hose, the fire was actually over and under them—blazing furiously in the floors both over their heads and under their feet. The firemen stubbornly fought from floor to floor, and had every time to retire.

The chief difficulty facing them was the large number of gas-pipes that ramified the establishment. All the smaller pipes quickly melted in the heat, and liberated gas which burst into flames and set fire to new portions of the building. Crowds of people were pressing round the fire and the firemen, whose operations they considerably hampered. All the hansom-cabs in London seemed to be making for Bayswater and the great spectacle; they stood in long rows blocking the main streets leading to Westbourne Grove and Queen's Road. News of the fire seemed to spread like magic through London. At Oxford Circus hansom-cabs were seen touting with cries and placards of "To Whiteley's Fire!" And as the flames leaped higher people who lived in the outer suburbs of London, at Acton, Ealing, Willesden, and Uxbridge, saw the blaze, harnessed carriages and carts, and drove off to be present at the spectacle.

The main disaster of the conflagration occurred before the fire had reached its most alarming proportions.

THE GREAT FIRE OF 1887
The wall falls and buries a fire-engine.
From *The Penny Illustrated Paper*

> The fire did not seem to be a large one, nor to have been burning long; but suddenly, without notice or alarm being given to the unfortunate people in the street, the great walls fell out and people were crushed and buried by the ruins. Great masses of brickwork knocked people down in all directions. . . . The vast mass of brickwork filled the roadway, and it suddenly dawned on the people round that the fire-engine was actually buried, and that there must be people buried too. . . . The firemen, by reason of their helmets and by other circumstances of good fortune which it is difficult to comprehend, had escaped being buried, and, managing to keep their feet, were able to move away from the spot with their lives. But the blows which they received had inflicted terrible injuries, and the intense heat had burned and scorched their faces. . . . Men all round, policemen and civilians, were doubled up with pain, or bleeding copiously from deep flesh wounds. And all this time the grave question was asked, how many people had been buried under the brickwork?

In the meantime the anxiously waiting fire authorities at Westminster and Southwark received the first definite news of the fire by telephone at 7.50, when the following message reached them:

> We find that Whiteley's manufacturing premises are well alight. A wall has fallen down, two of our men have been seriously injured and removed to hospital, and we are informed that there are people buried in the ruins.

This message indicated that the seriousness of the fire must be far greater than anything that had occurred in London since the great Tooley Street conflagration of 1861. Moreover, most of the previous great fires of London had broken out in the City, and it was something new to have a conflagration of this size in a residential area in the West End. The collapse of the wall gave rise to theories that the fire must have been aided by an explosion, presumably caused by incendiarism. When it fell, the flames naturally obtained a vent, and a loud, roaring noise could be heard from within. Many people supposed that only dynamite could account for such a violent collapse of masonry, while others reminded themselves of the huge stores of oil and spirit in the basement, which, they declared, must have burst through the heat of the conflagration.

The fire had now spread the entire length of Douglas Place, and was attacking the front buildings in Queen's Road. A large riding-school at the back, in Kensington Gardens Square, caught fire, and it seemed as if the firemen had lost all mastery of the outbreak. In Queen's Road all the window glass and frames were quickly destroyed, and through the great gaps which had been handsome windows that afternoon the gigantic furnace could be seen roaring and blazing. At half-past eight, when the roofs were burned through, the flames leaped still higher, and threw up a brilliant light which could be seen for miles all round London. Then at ten o'clock the central tower of the Queen's Road block with its flagstaff caught alight, and presented a magnificent appearance, swathed with dense clouds of black smoke and tongues of bright flame, which ascended to a level with the neighbouring church steeples. The sight, however, did not last long, for the tower soon fell with a crash into the burning abyss below.

By this time Captain Shaw, head of the Metropolitan Fire Brigade, had dispatched to the scene of the fire thirty-four steam fire-engines, six manuals, three hose-carts, four extension ladders, a coal-van, ninety-six horses, and 173 men. Messengers were running between the horse contractors and the stations to borrow more horses and coachmen to haul out more engines. The situation was complicated by other calls

QUEEN'S ROAD, BAYSWATER, ON SATURDAY, AUGUST 6, 1887
From *The Pall Mall Budget*, August 11, 1887

to fires which kept coming in from other districts in a most extraordinary manner.

It will illustrate the unprotected condition of all districts of London to state that steamers were at the Westbourne fire and at work from Brompton, Chelsea, Kensington, North Kensington, Paddington, Baker Street, Portland Road, Regent Street, Clerkenwell, Islington, St Luke's, Scotland Yard, Kentish Town, Holloway, Hackney, Mile End, Poplar, Shadwell, Bishopsgate, Shoreditch, Kennington, Tooley Street, Rotherhithe, Deptford, Old Kent Road,

> Greenwich, Camberwell, Brixton, Clapham, Battersea, Waterloo Road. . . . It is startling to think, with all these engines tied at the West End, what the results of a City or an East End outbreak would have been.

In point of fact, Whiteley's fire had monopolized thirty-four out of the forty-five steam fire-engines available for the whole of London, ninety-six out of the 131 horses, and 173 out of the 589 firemen. Nothing but a few score manual engines were left scattered through the rest of the Metropolis to meet other emergencies.

> At eleven o'clock the great fire may be said to have been at its height. All round the neighbourhood the steamers were standing busily pumping, and coal had to be requisitioned from all parts for their wants. . . . Every few minutes walls or floors fell in . . . at the centre of the premises with a roar resembling the discharge of artillery, and there were huge gaps left of shaking and bending walls which gave the ruins an extraordinary aspect. At the very height of the fire six firemen had the narrowest possible escape from instant death. One of the extension ladders had been thrown against a lofty building, and the upper or telescopic ladder was being made use of. Six men were standing on this length when there was a sudden burst of flame and the ladder caught fire. . . . It was only the foresight of the Chief Officer which saved the men's lives: he had given very strict instructions that there should always be foot-lashing to the ladders, and this alone held up the extension.
>
> The brickwork of the fallen wall was now cleared away and three bodies recovered. One was said to be that of Alfred Blake, the watchman of the premises. His wife, brought to identify the remains, at once said it was her husband and burst into tears. Her son also looked . . . and said, "I am sure it is not him; my father never wore a collar in his life." While they were disputing Blake himself entered the room.

VIEW OF THE FIRE OF 1887 AT ITS HEIGHT IN QUEEN'S ROAD

From *The Illustrated London News*

At last, towards three o'clock on the morning of the 7th, the firemen began to gain the upper hand. The waiting crowds, who had been solaced with supplies of cherries and ginger-beer distributed by a large horde of hawkers, now betook themselves to the many coffee-stalls which seemed to have mysteriously sprung

SKETCH OF WHITELEY MADE DURING HIS INTERVIEW WITH THE PRESS ON AUGUST 7, 1887
From *The Penny Illustrated Paper*, August 13, 1887

up in the offing. The flames and sparks died down. Soon there was nothing to see except smoke, nothing to hear except the hiss of water upon red-hot embers and ashes. An area of buildings 200 feet by 150 feet had been completely gutted. Three million gallons of water, drawn from the mains of the Grand Junction Waterworks Company, had been pumped on to the scene of the fire—enough to fill a reservoir twelve feet deep and an acre in extent. Worst of all was the loss of life, the number of killed being three. Sixteen people had been injured.

Whiteley reached Westbourne Grove at six o'clock on Sunday evening, and lost no time, first of all in inspecting the ruins, and subsequently in visiting the injured lying in St Mary's Hospital. He then returned to 31 Porchester Terrace, where, though he had had nothing to eat since the morning, he delayed his dinner in order to give an interview to a reporter from the Press Association. "He entered the room with a broad smile on his face," ran the report,

> and did not seem in the least disconcerted or disheartened by the stupendous loss he had undergone. So buoyant were his spirits that it drew forth comment. But to this Mr Whiteley laughingly replied that it was far better to encounter the reverse in fortune with a smile than with a downcast brow. Misfortune had dogged his footsteps since the first fire in November 1882 with a persistence that would have induced the great majority of men to give up the struggle in despair. But through all he had held on, not mourning over or looking back upon past losses, but rather with quickened energies pressing on to recoup those losses in the future.

Whiteley's own statement was marked by undismayed optimism:

> I came back fully prepared for the worst, but I scarcely thought matters would prove so bad as they have done. It is the most disastrous loss I have as yet sustained, and would paralyse most men. But I am not disheartened. I have inexhaustible energy and indomitable business pluck, and with the aid of these I do not doubt as to my ability to face this reverse, great though it may be. . . . By the fire which took place in June 1885, which was the last one, I was the loser of £350,000. Then I had only four shops burned out. Now practically seven have gone, and half a million of money, I am convinced, will not more than cover, even if it will cover, my loss. My counting-house has been burned

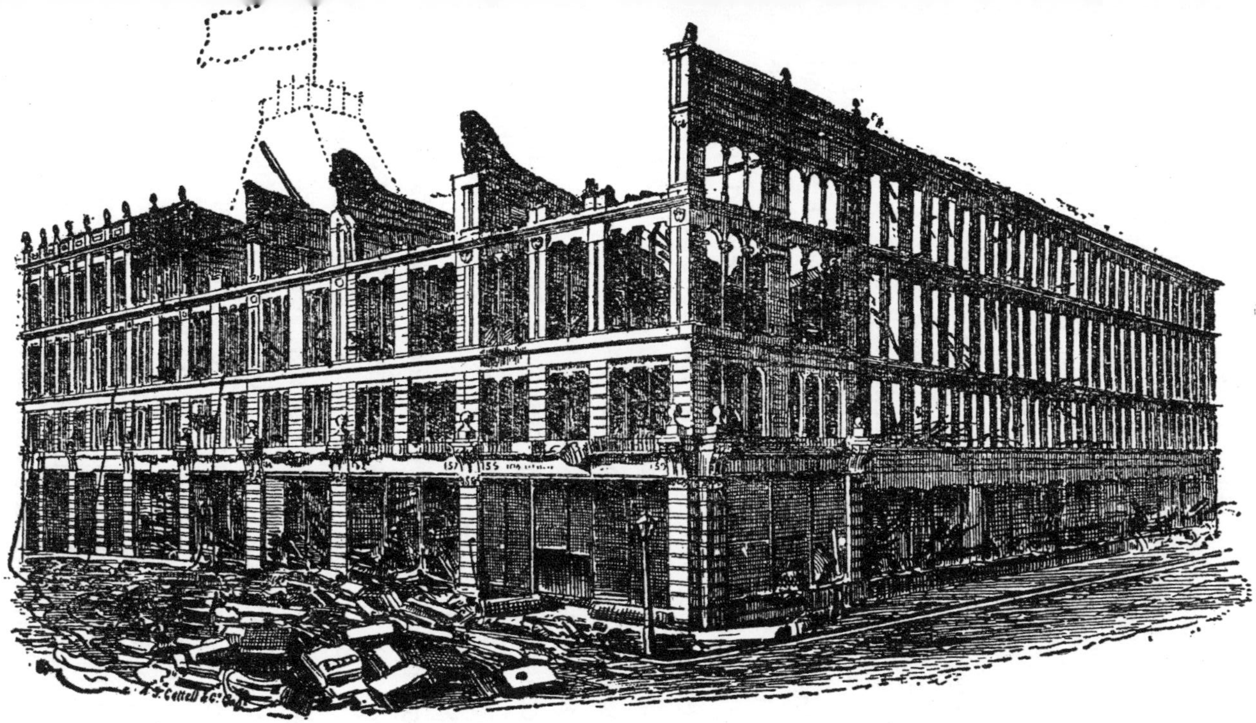

WHITELEY'S ON SUNDAY MORNING, AUGUST 7, 1887
From *The Bayswater Chronicle*, August 13, 1887

> out. We put all the important books in a strong-room at night; but in a business like mine it is impossible to put all the books in one place, and thus many of them must be inevitably lost. Then, again, we enter goods on the duplicate system, a duplicate being given to the customer; and the sales even for a single day must, of course, represent a very considerable sum of money.

Whiteley put his loss at £525,000, and added that the amount for which he was insured was "so small that it was practically worthless." He further explained, "You see, I have already had four fires, and to get insured under such circumstances I have found to be a matter of utmost difficulty; in fact, an impossibility." The Universal Provider declared himself firmly convinced that treachery or foul play had been responsible for the conflagration. He emphasized that his fires had always appeared to break out in twenty places at once, and that on this occasion the outbreak had been simultaneously observed on three different floors. "Some one," he said, "is animated by an animus against me."

Who the unknown villain could be who had so secretly and successfully set fire to these particular premises on so many separate occasions continued to agitate public opinion in London for several months. It was not possible even to begin to investigate the ruins for several days, as the fire went on smouldering till the morning of August 9. On that day Whiteley, accompanied by Keith, Burbidge, and Roche, as well as by a representative of the Metropolitan Board of Works, made a tour of the devastated buildings, from which the bodies of the victims were one by one being recovered. Though a thousand hands had been thrown out of work, Whiteley was able proudly to announce in a letter published that morning in *The Times* that

> notwithstanding the fire which took place in my Queen's Road premises on Saturday last is the most calamitous that has yet occurred, I have been enabled to complete arrangements for carrying on the business of every department without delay or inconvenience to my customers.

But though previous fires of the kind had not led to official inquiry, on this occasion, because of the loss of life, an inquest was necessary. This inquest the Middlesex Coroner held on August 10 and 17 at Westbourne Park Institute, and ultimately adjourned till October 24, for the purpose of seeing whether the reward of £2000 which Whiteley undertook to offer for information as to the source of the fire would evoke further evidence. Whiteley's own lieutenants rallied round their employer without delay, his buyers, headed by Burbidge, offering to subscribe £1000 from their own pockets in order to raise the reward from £2000 to £3000. Moreover, about a week after the fire the principal tradesmen of the Grove met together under the chairmanship of William Owen to consider the best means of expressing their sympathy with Whiteley in his disaster. After a speech by T. H. Ponting the meeting decided to frame and present an address of condolence to Whiteley, and to raise a subscription for the dependents of the victims of the fire.

Speculation as to the origin of the fire ranged over a wide field in the popular Press. An article entitled "Why is Whiteley's so often Burnt Down?" in the *Pall Mall Gazette* suggested three possible theories as to the fire's origin. The first (Whiteley's own theory) was that

> the fire is the work of some rival tradesman whom he has crushed under the juggernaut car of low prices and unlimited competition. The Universal Provider has risen into fame upon the universal destruction of all his rivals. Little tradesmen have gone down by the score in order that he might establish in the place of a hundred little shops his mammoth emporium.

But there were obvious practical objections to this theory, it being hardly possible to suppose that a small rival tradesman could have had the necessary access to, and complete knowledge of, the whole of Whiteley's premises to execute his nefarious task. The second, or romantic, theory was that

> the incendiary is some injured lady who seeks to assuage the fire that consumes her own heart by the spectacle of Whiteley's goods and chattels ascending to heaven in a flaming, fiery furnace.

The only support forthcoming for this theory was the fact that Whiteley was known to have been a ladies' man and to have become involved in matrimonial troubles. The third and most generally canvassed theory was that "the fire is due to some discontented employee who has some grudge against his master." An informant called upon the *Pall Mall Gazette* saying he had a relative employed under Whiteley. "The place," he said, "seethes with discontent. So far as I know, whether male or female, those who are employed by Whiteley regard their master with feelings of intense dislike. . . . His whole system is one of slave-driving from top to bottom. Whiteley himself patrols the establishment like a roaring lion. In my opinion it is a case for Parliament to interfere."

The publication of this article, which was widely reprinted, evoked a lively correspondence from employees and ex-employees of the Universal Provider, some declaring that the article was "one of the greatest lies that could be hurled against a good governor," and that they were "as happy and comfortable at Mr Whiteley's as at any other establishment" in which they had worked. The *Draper's Record*, on the other hand, admitted that

> there is reason to fear that Mr Whiteley does *not* treat his assistants with the amount of consideration they deserve. This year, for instance, he is understood to have laid it down as a rule that no assistant shall be paid for holidays at a higher rate than half-salary. This, so far as we are aware, is a regulation enforced in no other establishment upon old hands, and its operation has caused a good deal of heart-burning. At the same time it must be observed that a great deal of the soreness said to exist may arise from the fact that Mr Whiteley in the good times a few years ago paid higher salaries than any draper in London, and the economies dictated by the less profitable condition of business in these more degenerate days press all the more heavily upon assistants.

Naturally the Metropolitan Fire Brigade came in for severe criticism, particularly on account of the insufficiency of horses, which prevented full use being made of all the engines and escapes with which the various Metropolitan stations were equipped. As *Punch* sarcastically observed:

> There is no truth in the report that a whole brigade of firemen and sixteen fire-engines are now permanently encamped in Kensington Gardens Square, and that Captain

Shaw is about to take furnished lodgings in the immediate neighbourhood of Westbourne Grove. No, those men walking up and down the shop and eyeing everybody suspiciously are not shopwalkers, as you suppose! Four of them are detectives, with orders summarily to arrest any customer who looks at all like an incendiary, and the others are disguised firemen. . . . The fire-engine in the Hall is certainly a little in the way of the servants; with hydrants laid on to each floor, *and* sleeping in fireproof beds with one's clothes on, *and* having an outside iron staircase to each window in the house, we really *are* pretty safe against the next conflagration, in spite of the fact that we live just opposite a Universal Provider!

The inquest on the victims of the great fire, protracted as it was over three sessions and not closed till the end of October, threw no further light on the origin of the tragedy. Great efforts were made to investigate the supposed explosion which had caused the collapse of the wall and the three deaths which resulted from it. But after a good deal of evidence, mostly conflicting, the Chief Inspector under the Explosives Act declared himself unconvinced that there had been any explosion. In building-trade circles it was argued that the collapse of the walls was due to expansion through the heat of the iron girders used for the framework. But whatever the true origin was, even the huge reward offered by Whiteley did not induce any accomplice of the incendiary (if there had been one) to come forward and inform. Scotland Yard, indeed, examined over a hundred persons and followed up suggestions contained in numerous letters, both signed and anonymous. But in the end it had to be admitted that not one shred of real evidence had resulted. Accordingly the jury, after recording their opinion that the fire must have been wilfully caused by some person or persons possessing easy access to the premises, contented themselves with condemning the existing state of the law, which provided no machinery for the investigation of fires unless they had involved loss of life. They recommended—what afterwards became law—that every fire in the future should be officially investigated. Beyond this, and a suggestion made by the insurance companies that Whiteley's premises ought not to have housed in the same building manufacturing workshops and retail shops, no light was ever thrown upon the mystery. An epidemic of five great fires and several smaller fires had visited one single trader in a fashionable neighbourhood within the space of five years. If they were not due to accident, but were the result of deliberate planning, they provide perhaps the most famous example, together with the murders committed by Jack the Ripper, of a series of gigantic crimes carried through with impunity in the face of almost perfect precautions.

As on previous occasions, the Universal Provider somewhat overestimated the size of his monetary loss. His accounts, however, show how crippling the fire was to his economy. The total loss amounted to £153,715, of which £80,000 represented premises, £20,000 fixtures, and the balance stock. Against this he had only the poor consolation of some £4000 or £5000 recovered from a number of small insurance companies, chiefly Continental and American. The damage done to his trade was nearly as serious as the capital damage. The accounts for the year ending February 29, 1888, showed a loss on the year's trading of £131,135—so that had there been no fire Whiteley would have made a net profit of £52,000 that year, a sum considerably smaller than in 1887. How did he meet this gigantic loss? Partly by borrowing from his customers (sundry creditors, including bank deposits, rose from £243,000 to £325,000 in that year), partly from his bankers in the form of an overdraft of £32,000, and partly in the form of a loan of £30,000 from the contractors who undertook the rebuilding of the destroyed premises. This substantial debt—far the largest which Whiteley had ever been involved in—was not liquidated for several years. In the accounts for 1888–89 the volume of creditors had risen to £375,000, which included bank deposits amounting to £138,000 and a bank loan of £50,000; the loan from the contractors had been paid off—or, rather, absorbed by the other creditors. A year later we find that the bank loan had also been discharged, but bank deposits had risen to £190,000. In the long run, therefore, Whiteley succeeded in financing his fire losses on this occasion by borrowing more money from his customers.

CHAPTER VI

The Golden Age

HALF in admiration, half in joke, the *Bayswater Chronicle* watched "the Bayswater Phœnix" rise from the ashes and preen its wings anew. It described the scene that autumn (1887) thus:

> Far into the late nocturnal hours in the gleams and weird shadows of the meteoric electric light, and throughout the dun November day, Mr Whiteley's grand new pile in the Queen's Road rises on the former ruins. It is a race against time. The Provider for the Universe . . . has pledged himself to reopen in Queen's Road by Christmas. Hence the sound of clanking chains, hoarse voices, and heavy timbers till near midnight, when the lieges should all be asleep.

On December 8 the provision department was opened on the ground floor, and by the third week of February 1888 traces of the fire had almost vanished, the scaffolding was being removed from the façade of a fine new row of shops, and the famous clock was being re-erected over the heads of the passers-by. True, the Christmas takings—usually reckoned at £15,000 a day—were sadly shrunken, but opportunity was taken to prepare to recoup the loss during the following winter by opening a new and enlarged toy department, which in fact proved such an attraction as to achieve sales worth £12,000 during 1888. In his new buildings Whiteley determined to adopt precautions which would render any large-scale outbreak of fire impossible for the future. A system of metal pipes perforated with holes was installed, through which water could be discharged in copious showers. These pipes ran along the ceiling of every room on every floor, so that by the turning of a single cock one department or all the departments in a building could be flooded with water. Fortunately no occasion for their use arose. If the fire of 1887 was the work of an incendiary, it was his last effort! No doubt the odds in favour of discovery had grown too great to risk. The whole establishment was on its toes to prevent another fire, and when in June 1888 a match was accidentally dropped in the trunk department it was not the match, but a hand-grenade thrown by a zealous assistant to extinguish it, that made two holes in the carpet, and caused the spread of rumours of "another fire at Whiteley's" round the neighbourhood! But the danger was over. The great emporium was no more troubled by this particular kind of disaster. And, said the *Bayswater Chronicle*, "no one but a disappointed incendiary will grudge Mr Whiteley his Phœnix-like resurrection."

Nevertheless, in more ways than one the position of the Universal Provider was different after the conflagrations from what it had been before. Whiteley's opinions and actions had the same 'news value' to the Press as ever, but his personality was treated with more respect and sympathy. The newspapers were quick to publish his views on public affairs—on the proposed taxes on carts and champagne in the Budget of 1888, for instance. Next year the rumour that he was contemplating starting branches in other parts of London, particularly the Holloway Road, brought a characteristic interview with a reporter.

"They say, Mr Whiteley, you are going to be more universal than ever?"

"Do they? As a rule they know my business sooner than I do myself, and it is so in this case. This is the first I hear about the Holloway affair. I would sooner think of establishing a branch at Bombay or Calcutta than at Holloway. If the Holloway people want to buy my goods they can come to Westbourne Grove. The truth is, I am against branches, for I believe in the master's eye being everywhere, and I have hardly enough eyes to keep this place straight. This very day I have discovered that for the last three years I have been cheated at the rate of fifteen pounds a week, and with all my supervision I have not discovered it sooner."

Again, in the summer of 1892 a rumour that Whiteley was about to vacate the whole of his twenty shops in Westbourne Grove and move elsewhere, on account of his landlord's attempt to raise rents on the expiration of his leases, caused "something of a panic" in the locality, and led to a Press correspondence, in the course of which stress was laid on Whiteley's economic value to Bayswater. Gone were the days when he was pilloried for 'unfair competition' with his smaller rivals.

In fact, a certain change was coming over the conduct of the business. As early as 1888 it began to be remarked that the Universal Provider's prices were no longer the lowest on the market. A new North Country provision dealer who had established himself on the north side of the Grove forced every grocer in the neighbourhood, including Whiteley, to lower the price of butter by twopence a pound. A housekeeper, writing to the *Bayswater Chronicle*, remarks:

It used to be thought by some innocent people that Mr

> Whiteley had touched the lowest prices, as regards provisions, but now "the cat's out of the bag"—Mr Whiteley has evidently been making a fairly good profit out of us.

The discovery was hailed as a revolution that

> cannot fail to emphasize the distinction that already exists—with a few exceptions—between the south, aristocratic and pleasurable, and the north, popular and businesslike, sides of the Westbournia thoroughfare.

Later a newcomer from the country, settling for the first time in Bayswater, was to notice that the little shopkeeper had begun to undersell the big shopkeeper once more. She wrote:

> Bessie of Guernsey, of mature experience, had advised me to get everything at Whiteley's. "You've only got to walk into the shop, order what you want in the different departments, and you find everything delivered at your door!" She was right, but I soon found that this easy way of buying had to be paid for by too high prices, so I determined to explore the neighbourhood, buy what I wanted, and bring it home myself. . . . In an old, narrow, winding lane, once no doubt a medieval thoroughfare, I found shops and stalls catering for those who have no money to waste and mean to get the utmost value for their outlay. They were not to be put off with stale vegetables or doubtful fish—such as I had experienced in the 'better-class' shops.

Whiteley, indeed, continued to display much of his old sense of enterprise and publicity, but in ways rather less objectionable to other tradesmen. Now he would exhibit a special travelling palanquin, containing "all the comforts of a Pullman car," which he had built for the use of a lady explorer who intended to cross unknown Africa. Now he would open in Kensington Gardens Square a handsomely furnished reading-room, luxuriously carpeted, where for a penny his customers could read all the papers of the day. Now he would provide an orchid display, show Linnell's picture of *Bayswater Forty Years Ago*, establish a lost-property office for his customers, or exhibit his bulldog "King Orry," the champion of All England, who would hold a daily levee in Westbourne Grove for dog-lovers from all parts of London. Only three new enterprises likely to upset other traders were attempted during the next ten years. The first, undertaken in 1888, was the retailing of milk. After three years Whiteley obtained a supply direct from Buckinghamshire and sold it, not in small quantities, but on a subscription system (twenty-four pint-tickets for four shillings) to his regular customers. A year later one of the largest dairy companies in West London had, at its annual meeting, to report a reduced dividend because "the whole of the dairy business had been disorganized by the price reduction of fivepence to fourpence a quart." But Whiteley discontinued his milk department in 1897, ostensibly because of his disapproval of the Sunday work it involved.

His second competitive enterprise was in laundry. In 1892 he purchased four acres of land in Avonmore Road, near Earl's Court, and bored a well six hundred feet deep in order to obtain his own water-supply. At first only a few families patronized the service, until Whiteley hit upon the device—which went straight to the heart of Kensington snobs—of segregating servants' washing from that of the rest of the family, marking it in blue with special labels and packing it separately. In the same district he also built a block of lofty warehouses, with lifts and electric lighting, to house the forage department and a furniture repository.

His third enterprise was in transport. The part of London from which Whiteley thought he saw a chance of attracting more custom was North London, an area which, however, was particularly inaccessible from Bayswater. To remedy this deficiency Whiteley approached the London General Omnibus Company, and invited them to run a service of buses from Camden Town to Bayswater. The company declared the proposal uneconomic, and refused to run a service, but added that if anyone else did so they would start a service of their own in competition. This was just the sort of reply likely to provoke the Universal Provider. He immediately planned a twelve-minute service of his own, to run from Camden Town past the Zoo, through St John's Wood and Warwick Road, to the Bayswater Road, at a fare of fourpence. No sooner said than done. Other tradesmen in the district supported him in his scheme. So punctually at ten o'clock in the morning of April 1, 1895, the first bus, gay with chocolate body and yellow wheels, and conspicuously labelled "To Whiteley's" and "To Owen's," drove down Porchester Road and discharged a bevy of fashionable shoppers at the entrance to the Grove. Ten buses were employed on the service, eight of which Whiteley had specially built. The enterprise, however, did not endure beyond the point of spurring the L.G.O.C. into action.

None of these enterprises provoked any serious reactions from his fellow-tradesmen, though he was involved in four years' litigation with a firm that disapproved of his functions as banker—a case that was ended only by a House of Lords decision in 1892. As time passed his fondness for the law-courts seemed to increase rather than decline. During the early nineties he was as busy as ever prosecuting shoplifters and delinquent employees and customers—sometimes, however, receiving a rap over the knuckles when he exceeded his rights. Twice he was fined for selling short weight, and once he was unsuccessfully blackmailed by a man and woman who occupied one of his lodging-houses in Queen's Road. Occasionally he had tiffs with his fellow-tradesmen—as when he refused the request of the Early Closing Association to join Ponting's and Owen's in shutting all shops for an extra day at Christmas 1892, when the festival fell on a Sunday. But he more than regained his lost popularity by championing the cause of a new cheap material, 'flannelette,' whose appearance on the market in 1894 led to Whiteley's prosecution for a breach of the Merchandise Marks Act. The action which followed proved a 'test' case, to determine whether the term 'flannelette' might be used or not. The course of the case afforded Whiteley a typical opportunity to display his cunning. During the long hearing the magistrate had two rolls of material, one of flannel and the other of flannelette, placed on either side of him. At one moment he forgot which was which, and permitted himself to make some very complimentary remarks about the quality of the flannelette, thinking he was referring to the genuine flannel. Whiteley's counsel was about to interrupt and correct the magistrate, when the astute man of business prevented him, and allowed his Worship to proceed with his eulogy. At its conclusion Whiteley rose and urbanely thanked the magistrate for the tribute he had been paying to the qualities of the article he had been selling. The laughter that followed can be imagined, and it did not take many more sittings of the court before Whiteley won the day. So pleased were the textile manufacturers of the North of England with his victory that they made him a presentation in the form of a cheque, a massive silver cup, and an illuminated address of thanks.

The obverse side of the picture was an occasional outbreak of labour trouble. Thus in October 1895 the journeymen tailors whom he employed went on strike, in protest against his decision, on account of bad trade, to reduce their wages below sixpence (and in some cases to threepence) an hour. The strike lasted three months, and received active support from Lady Dilke and other opponents of 'sweating.' On November 5 the strikers marched in procession through the streets of Paddington with band and banners, evoking old memories of Guy Fawkes' Day in 1876 by parading an effigy of the Universal Provider on horseback in their midst. But in those days it had been the tradesmen who showed their hatred of him; now it was the wage-earners—significant sign of changed times!

The Universal Provider was now in his sixties—an age when most men are thinking of retirement rather than a new start. But Whiteley, having translated into reality the dream of his dawning manhood, now began to seek fulfilment of an earlier dream still, a dream of his boyhood. For before he had been a draper's apprentice he had been a farmer's boy. Before he had seen the Crystal Palace he had known the love of the land; and underneath the outer trading man there still lurked the inner labouring man—expressed in his love of horses and dogs, of racing and open-air sports, of flowers, fruit, and vegetables. Now that he had carried his great shopkeeping enterprise through to prosperity, and there were no more rivals to remove, no more fires to defy, no more rebellious servants to crush, he began to plan something new. In England farming was in a bad way. Farmers could no longer make a living, so it was said. Well, thought Whiteley, that is because the methods are wrong, the scale of production is inadequate, the capital employed is too mean. He knew that he had made a success of his own business by daring to combine many branches of trade and enlarging the scope of his operations beyond what other men envisaged. Why not apply these principles, so successful in trade, to the business of farming? Once more the patriarchal instinct rose strong within him. He would show England what a successful man of business could do by applying the factory system to a backward industry. Better still, he would make that industry subserve his main trade; the farm should feed the shop, and both together benefit the customer through cheaper prices for food of high quality and freshness.

In the spring of 1890 Whiteley determined to establish a flower farm and a strawberry farm for the purpose of supplying his own shops. Soon he became famous for his orchids, which won prizes when they were exhibited by the Royal Horticultural Society. In the next year he extended his operations more widely. A drive of an hour and a quarter from Bayswater along the Uxbridge Road brought one in those days out into open country, a rich and fruitful alluvial plain, full of gardens, orchards, and trees. In the midst of this was the village of Hillingdon,

Middlesex, where Whiteley established his new farm —or, as he chose to have it called, his "fruit and flower factory." It occupied eleven acres of ground, surrounded by a wall fifteen feet high. Inside were several buildings—a large square water-tower, stables, and five or six pretty gardeners' cottages. The ground was divided into two parts—one occupied by greenhouses and sheds, the other by crops. In July 1891 a representative of the *Bayswater Chronicle*, conducted round the farm by Whiteley in person, noted that

> after acting as attentive guide and interpreter for four or five hours he [Whiteley] leaves you with all the freshness, politeness, and suavity with which he began. He is blessed with a splendid physique, with a giant strength in a square-set, well-knit frame.

Everything was on a lavish and first-class scale—the orchid-house, the vinery (672 feet long), the palm-house (270 feet long), the mushroom-house, and the special system of irrigation by water-tanks and steam-engine.

> The Universal Provider, though by no means a nervous man, would absolutely shudder at the sight of a single superficial foot of unoccupied space.

But the Hillingdon estate did not long satisfy his ambition. Before the year 1891 was out he had purchased more land nearer the Thames at Hanworth, just north of Hampton Court. This estate was of 200 acres, comprising two farms called Butt's and Glebe. As much of the land was occupied with trees, his first step was to cut them down, clear the ground, and plant "a forest of fruit-trees"—which included over 14,000 apple-trees, 30,000 gooseberry-bushes, a quarter of a million raspberry-canes, and three-quarters of a

VIEW OF WHITELEY'S MODEL FARM AND FACTORIES AT HILLINGDON

From *Orchards and Gardens*

million strawberry-plants. A staff of 150 planters was engaged to look after the fruit-trees, and Whiteley planned and designed a set of cottages to accommodate them, provided them with a lecture hall and recreation ground, and then built himself a small bungalow in their midst. The purpose of this vast plantation was to produce material for jams, pickles, and other dainty comestibles; and the whole establishment, as an observer described it, was "a fit exemplification of the factory system applied to agriculture." During the pickling season 300 pickers were employed daily, starting work at four in the morning and earning from 2*s.* 6*d.* to 3*s.* 6*d.* a day. With the fruit so gathered Whiteley intended to prove that pure jam could be made cheaply. He had it picked, simmered in immense copper pans, and bottled all in a continuous process at the rate of 1800 bottles an hour. Hygiene ruled everywhere. Each utensil was cleansed by steam and rinsed out with filtered water.

> The workmen, in their clean shirts, white caps and aprons, are quite pictures of propriety, whilst the women, in their dainty print skirts and white blouses, are equally admirable.

In a week the staff could turn out preserves to the value of £1500. There was also a bee-farm with fifty hives, a vegetable garden, many hothouses, and six mushroom-houses.

The other half of the 'food factory' was concerned with animal products. There was a herd of cows, whose milk (totalling 1200 gallons a week) was dispatched twice daily to Westbourne Grove. There were model piggeries with a new kind of patent trough specially designed by Whiteley himself. He never kept less than 500 pigs, all of the Berkshire breed. There was a set of kennels in which almost every kind of dog was bred, including Marco, a great Dane, which won the prize at Cruft's in 1893. There was also a poultry farm, including pigeons, and a rabbit warren. Finally in 1894 Whiteley added to the Hanworth farms an adjacent property called the Rookeries Estate (thirty-four acres), which he quickly transformed from "an ancient and beautifully wooded demesne," with tennis-courts, stables, and ornamental lawns, into a vast and productive turnip-field.

Meanwhile the workpeople on the estate, over 400 in number, were accommodated in a model village with two streets of cottages and several blocks of villas. They had a medical officer of their own, as well as sick-benefit clubs—all provided by Whiteley. A small staff of specialists was employed to deal with the scientific aspects of the business—among them the analyst of the Paddington Vestry, whose job it was to ensure that no dirt could be introduced or adulteration take place in the food. The 'factory' turned out various specialities for which Whiteley's provisions department became famous—beef-tea lozenges, for instance, of which it was said that "a box of these nutritious tablets would keep a man alive for a week," real turtle soup, made from turtles imported from the West Indies and brought alive to the farm turtle-pens, and mock-turtle soup, made from calves' heads.

Whiteley was so proud of his farms that he determined to immortalize their glories in print. During 1895 he commissioned a writer named Alfred Barnard to compile a complete account of the whole enterprise, and to illustrate it lavishly with photographs and drawings. At Christmas 1895 he arranged with Sir Joseph Causton and Sons to publish it in a volume under the title *Orchards and Gardens.* He himself took 50,000 copies, and stocked his windows and counters with piles of them, offered at five shillings apiece. But his expectations were sadly disappointed. Few copies were bought, and the work proved a dead loss to him.

In fact, the Hanworth and Hillingdon farms were constructed on far too lavish a scale, and were run with far too elaborate methods ever to pay their way. Their products were mostly of fine quality, but were more costly than those to be found in the open market. The Universal Provider, however, was set on feeding his provision-shops from his farms. He expected these departments to buy from Hanworth and Hillingdon meat, vegetables, fruit, jam, and pickles at prices remunerative to the farms, and to sell them on the counter as cheap as the public could buy them elsewhere. But this was impossible, and therefore Whiteley's buyers for these departments were always on the horns of a dilemma. Their employer was annoyed with them if they bought stock elsewhere, but also annoyed if they failed to sell what they bought from his farms. And so trouble crept in—as, for example, in 1894 when carcasses of pigs infected with swine fever were found at the farm ready dressed for sending to Westbourne Grove, and Whiteley was fined twenty pounds for an offence of which he was personally ignorant.

Yet, though the Hanworth and Hillingdon experiments turned out costly failures, Whiteley did not devote to them so much attention as to distract him altogether from his main business of shopkeeping. The great emporium in Westbourne Grove and Queen's Road had, indeed, reached about the limit of its expansion, employing some 6000 hands. Its prices were no longer as low as they had been in the seventies or eighties, and new competitors were springing up on every side—either great departmental stores, like Harrod's, launched in 1889, or multiple shops specializing in a few lines of goods or services, such as Lipton's or the Home and Colonial Stores. Yet the demand of the consumer kept pace with all these efforts to supply his needs, and Whiteley's prosperity seemed greater than ever. Never had there been more calls upon the services of Whiteley's hire department, which took on more frequent and more magnificent functions. In March 1889 Whiteley managed the Charity Ice Carnival at the Albert Hall, which was opened by the Duchess of Teck and visited by the Queen. Three thousand guineas was taken at the door, one third of which Whiteley retained for his own expenses and profit. Five months later, in August, he ran a paddle-steamer and special train for guests to see the Naval Review at Spithead. Then in October he undertook the catering arrangements for the opening of Mansfield College, Oxford, and fed 600 guests in a gigantic marquee. During 1892 he was occupied with fitting out and decorating the first of the modern spectacular exhibitions at Olympia, Imre Kiralfy's "Venice in London."[1] The same year he began a series of undertakings for Indian princes, the first of whom was the Gaekwar of

[1] It is said that the chairs supplied by Whiteley for this exhibition were, at its close, taken over by the company which in 1894 began to fill London with Lyons' teashops.

FRUIT-PICKERS AT WORK ON WHITELEY'S MODEL STRAWBERRY FARM

From *Orchards and Gardens*

Baroda, who had come to London for the wedding of Prince George and Princess Mary in June 1893. The Gaekwar entrusted Whiteley with the task of buying a wedding present costing £700 for the Royal pair, and out of gratitude for his services presented a silver cup to be competed for by the Kildare Athletic Club at their annual sports. Whiteley was invited to decorate the streets of the City of London for the wedding, but had to decline in order to concentrate his resources on a still more important task—the decoration of St James's Street and the exterior of St James's Palace. The Princess, who had for several years past employed Whiteley to supply works of taste and *bric-à-brac* for her household, expressed satisfaction with his decorations, which consisted chiefly of festoons, flowers, velvet, and flags.

In 1895 another picturesque visitation to Westbourne Grove was made by Nasrulla Khan, the Shahzada of Afghanistan, who with his suite made large purchases of silks, embroideries, rifles, and pistols at Whiteley's. During the next few years the firm's shipping department did an active business sending goods out to India, one of the largest enterprises undertaken being the supply to Prince Morvi of a whole railway and a fleet of steamboats. Whiteley boasted that most of the Rajahs and Maharajahs were customers of his, buying for their Courts dresses, table delicacies, wines, and amusements.

These years were also years of gigantic catering enterprises. For instance, in 1895 Whiteley undertook to feed 26,000 people who attended the harvest festival organized by Hugh Macalmont, owner of the famous racehorse Isinglass, at his country seat near Newmarket. Then in August of the following year, 1896, he was called upon to cater for 15,000 guests on each of two days during a pageant at Fountains Abbey organized by Ripon Town Council. Two hundred waiters were sent north, with a quantity of food greater than was actually needed. In a speech during the festivities the Bishop of Ripon publicly thanked Whiteley, and referred to him as "Whiteley—of the Universe."

Still greater compliments were paid him about the same time when he undertook the arrangements for the marriage of Princess Maud, which included decorating Buckingham Palace, the Royal Chapel, the streets through which the wedding procession passed, and the gardens where 14,000 guests were received at the wedding party. The *Bayswater Chronicle* observed:

> It is no secret that Her Majesty was especially well pleased with the aspect Mr Whiteley put upon things at Buckingham Palace Gardens. It was done with such good judgment and excellent pictorial effects as to draw from Her Majesty the exclamation, "What, are *these* my gardens?" The very gracious commendation of the Bayswater William Whiteley followed. As a result Mr Whiteley had an intimation from the Lord Chamberlain requesting a visit from him. The Queen was so much pleased that she would like Mr Whiteley to have her Royal Warrant as General Furnisher to Her Majesty.

The Queen

> had never before given this mark of her own favour unsolicited, and its bestowal as a spontaneous action was a special and flattering acknowledgment of his services at the Royal Wedding.

The Warrant was framed and hung in Whiteley's picture gallery in Queen's Road.

During the autumn of the same year Whiteley

capped his exploits by undertaking the decoration of Nelson's Column on Trafalgar Day. In the whole of the South of England no steeplejack could be found daring enough to ascend to the top, so a jack had to be brought down from the North, who climbed up, decorated the statue with laurel, and then twined the entire column with laurel wreaths. This achievement added immensely to Whiteley's kudos, and established him as unrivalled in the art of public decoration. All that year, in spite of his attention to public functions, the Universal Provider continued to develop the efficiency of his retail business. Though he no longer undersold his fellow-tradesmen in Westbourne Grove and Queen's Road, he was quick to retaliate if others tried to steal a march upon him along the same road. A newly arrived draper, for instance, who thought to create a sensation by offering dress shirts at 25 per cent. reduction—to the disgust of his neighbours—found himself speedily thwarted by Whiteley, who at once filled his windows with similar goods at a still lower price. That summer Hyde Park was opened for the first time to cyclists—and an immense impetus was given to the popular craze for bicycling, which was then spreading, particularly among women. Whiteley took advantage of the fashion, ordered a large stock of machines, and sold them for thirteen pounds apiece—on the hire-purchase system if necessary. Another new development that year, which amazed his competitors, was his provision of a daily delivery service free for the benefit of his customers in Brighton.

Whiteley also retained as strongly as ever his fondness for participating in the domestic affairs of his customers. The well-known humorist F. Anstey, in a play contributed to *Punch* in 1893 entitled *The Man from Blankley's*,[1] represented the Universal Provider as supplying guests on hire to fill vacant seats at dinner-parties. The origin of this story can be traced to 1891, when the *Pall Mall Gazette*, hearing that Whiteley was doing business in this peculiar field at a charge of a guinea a head per evening, sent a special lady commissioner to investigate in Westbourne Grove. She commenced her task by adopting the name of Jenkinson, and writing to Whiteley as follows:

> Mrs Jenkinson has been told by several lady friends that Mr Whiteley occasionally supplies guests for parties. Will Mr Whiteley kindly tell Mrs Jenkinson whether this is correct? Mrs Jenkinson is giving a party on Tuesday next, and would be glad to secure the services of two or three well-educated gentlemen to act as stopgaps.

Immediately there came back a reply:

> Mr Whiteley presents his compliments to Mrs Jenkinson, and in reply to her letter begs to state he will be very pleased to furnish any gentlemen required for her party, and the fee for each one would be 21*s*. He will be glad to hear by return of post how many will be wanted.

The lady commissioner now pressed home her request:

> Mrs Jenkinson will call on Mr Whiteley on Monday afternoon to arrange about the gentlemen for her party. Mrs Jenkinson would like if possible to see the gentlemen. Unless they are fairly young, and able to talk and dance well, she fears it would be no use engaging them.

In due course the lady commissioner visited the Universal Provider, and found herself in the presence of a

[1] The play became a popular success when produced on the stage, and has been frequently revived since, the last time being in 1930.

bald-headed greybeard who played the part of showman to the young gentlemen who were brought out for inspection. First came a dapper, nice-looking little man on the right side of thirty. Asked if he was an accomplished dancer, Mr Sunning said, "I think I dance fairly well. I was at a Cinderella dance last week, and a ball at the Eyre Arms, and a——"

"Then I am sure, Mr Sunning, you will be a great acquisition to my party. Gentlemen who dance well are so very scarce. I shall expect you to rescue as many wallflowers as possible."

Next came a gallant-looking young fellow with a bronzed face and luxuriant moustache, with interesting scars on his face. He had served in the Hussars and been in India, offered to wear uniform if necessary, and to tell the ladies amusing anecdotes.

The third did not impress the lady commissioner favourably. He was a rather sheepish-looking youth, wearing a frock-coat much too large for him; and though he claimed to be able to dance the cotillon well, he was rejected for his careless appearance. The showman assured 'Mrs Jenkinson' that all candidates had dress clothes and would present visiting-cards.

A facility which went even beyond this singular provision of stopgap guests was offered by Whiteley in 1895. He caused to be inserted in the editorial columns of the *Bayswater Chronicle* the amazing suggestion that his lady customers could not do better than turn over to him the management of their finances.

> "I've no time for accounts," said the Duchess of —— the other day to the Marquis of ——, "and they're an awful bother!"
>
> "But why not do as I do?" replied the Marquis.

" What's that ? " said the Duchess.

" Why, turn them over to Whiteley," was the reply. " He'll keep them for you, and send you a statement whenever you choose to wire for it—at a moment's notice. He has kept my wife's accounts for years, and can even tell her how many dusters she ought to have in the house, and where they are ! It saves her a world of trouble. You couldn't do better ! "

" I'll do it," said the Duchess. And she is now one of a number of titled and society people who do the same.

The idea does not seem so absurd when we consider that many families of humbler rank were not ashamed to use Whiteley as a kind of family solicitor. One day one of his customers came to the Universal Provider and explained to him that he was very much worried about the conduct of his two daughters, who seemed to be gadding about town and might be falling into mischief. He commissioned Whiteley to investigate their behaviour, and see if he could account for their actions. No commission could be more acceptable. Whiteley at once entrusted to his chief costs clerk the confidential mission of shadowing the two girls wherever they went and finding out what they were doing. This difficult job lasted a whole month. Every day the clerk had to present himself to Whiteley on the stroke of nine in the morning in his house in Porchester Terrace, and give him personally a full report of the two girls' movements throughout the preceding day, for transmission to their father. But in fact he found that they did little else than walk, walk, walk, all day round the West End, in Hammersmith, Fulham, and Kensington. He was unable to find anything suspicious or improper in their behaviour—so their father was disappointed of his odd suspicions.

Given sufficient custom, no doubt Whiteley would have been glad to open a matrimonial agency. A customer once remarked to the Universal Provider that he seemed able to supply everything except one thing. "What is that?" asked the shopkeeper. "A wife," came the reply. Thereupon Whiteley carried the customer off to one of his departments, beckoned forward an attractive-looking female assistant who stood behind the counter, and introduced the two. Each was taken with the other, and a few months later Whiteley officiated at their wedding, and gave the girl away to his customer.

The Queen's Diamond Jubilee in 1897 provided Whiteley with a fresh opportunity of advertising his powers of display. That spring he flooded London with an array of Jubilee souvenirs, including a china mug which was said to have taken the fancy of almost every member of the Royal Family, as well as of some members of Lord Salisbury's Government. This mug carried a medallion of the Queen, flanked by representations of Westminster Palace, Balmoral, and Windsor Castle, and on the obverse the latest types of ironclad in the British Navy. As the day of celebration approached Whiteley joined with his fellow-tradesmen in a petition to the Queen to include Westbourne Grove in the route to be followed by her carriage when she visited Kensington on June 28. Though the petition was rejected, the Queen visited Paddington instead on June 21, and all Bayswater was decorated and illuminated for the occasion. This time Whiteley's was gay after dark as well as by day—a sign that the fear of fire was banished. Not only did he decorate his shops with a double festoon of green foliage running the full length of his buildings, but at nightfall his front was spangled with fiery stars which picked out monograms surrounding a colossal Royal Arms.

> As a specimen of bold, simple decoration, not frittered away in detail, these pictures in 'fire and foliage' were very successful, and were much applauded from the garden seats of the omnibuses which rolled by until a late hour.

Whiteley's principal feat in the Jubilee celebrations, however, was the decorating of the offices of the Royal Insurance Company in St James's Street; here he achieved a startling result by covering the whole building from the pavement to the second floor with vertical strips of pink and white material carefully box-pleated. This was surmounted by a burnished copper inscription which read: "Thou art alone the Queen of Earthly Queens."

After the Jubilee Whiteley's services as caterer were in greater demand than ever. During 1898 he undertook contracts in Birmingham, Manchester, and Edinburgh, and supplied two miles of chairs to seat the spectators who attended the opening of Blackwall Tunnel. Another commission was to take charge of a party of fifty visitors from Hawarden who came to London for three days in June to attend Gladstone's funeral. Again, when the sanitary conditions of the barracks at Windsor were found to be so unsatisfactory as to necessitate the removal of the Life Guards to a camp in Windsor Great Park, it was Whiteley who contracted to provide the tents and provisions for them. He also provided 5000 horses for service in the Cavalry manœuvres on Salisbury Plain. To meet the rush of work which this entailed upon his hire department he was forced to acquire a row of stables in Moscow Road for use as warehouses in which to store the necessary equipment and paraphernalia.

But the time was now at hand when the burden of sole responsibility for directing this vast enterprise was becoming too heavy even for a Universal Provider. Whiteley was in his sixty-eighth year, and was growing stouter and less active. His two sons, Frank and William, had entered the business in 1889, and since 1893, when the former had come of age, both had taken an increasingly active part in the work, especially on its financial side. They were, indeed, hardly old enough to manage the vast concern by themselves, nor was Whiteley ready to do more than share his power. But he noticed that other large shopkeeping businesses had recently followed the example set by Harrod's and turned themselves into joint-stock companies. Thus in 1891 Maple's, in 1894 Lyons', and in 1895 the International Stores had each taken this step. Finally in 1898 Sir Thomas Lipton, a close personal friend of Whiteley, also converted his 245 shops into a company, and so set the latter a decisive example. There were also one or two minor personal setbacks about this time, which may have contributed to make the Universal Provider weary of sole power. In the autumn of 1897 he had thrown himself into supporting a scheme for extending Westbourne Grove to the west, by constructing a new thoroughfare across Bayswater to Shepherd's Bush, which would have doubled the importance of the Grove as a shopping centre by making it easily accessible to the growing suburbs of Acton and Ealing. The idea was brilliant, but the obstacles from other interests proved too great, and the scheme fell through.[1] Then during the next year his oldest customer—that Mrs Johnson who thirty-five years earlier had prayed for his success on the day he had opened his first shop—died. And that autumn he, who had driven horses without a single accident for nearly sixty years, found himself involved in a collision at the corner of Queen's Road between his phaeton and a runaway horse and cart. Neither Whiteley nor the lady he was driving was hurt, but he was shaken by the accident, and the damage to his phaeton was ill requited by the prosecution and fining of the cart-driver, who was charged with " furious driving." Lastly, early in 1899 he was annoyed by the echoes of an old controversy, in the form of a dispute between a contractor he was employing and the clerk to the Paddington Vestry over the construction of a new sewer between Moscow Road and Salem Gardens. But neither side wanted a repetition of the old squabble, and the affair was adjusted when Whiteley agreed to conform to the regulations of the Vestry.

For many years past it had been Whiteley's custom to provide an annual banquet in November at the Cecil Hotel or the Savoy for his friends and principal employees. Seven or eight hundred guests would assemble, including notabilities from the City or Parliament, to hear Whiteley exchange compliments and reminiscences with his manager, James Keith, or utter his sentiments on the latest development in trade. The Universal Provider added to his other gifts a capacity for speaking well in public: his voice was pleasant and clear, his speech fluent and precise, and his manner

[1] This scheme evidently gave G. K. Chesterton his idea for the central episode in *The Napoleon of Notting Hill*.

placable and courteous. At the dinner in 1898 he combined an appeal to his fellow-tradesmen to shorten the hours of work of their employees with a reference to the forthcoming reorganization of his own business. And soon after Christmas these hints began to take concrete shape. Whiteley's, it was said, was to be transformed into a limited company, with seven directors (including Keith, himself, and his two sons), and an issue of debenture, preference, and ordinary shares to the public. The last piece of news roused considerable excitement in financial circles. It was believed that the firm had been earning very large profits, and that the investing public would snatch eagerly at any opportunity to share in them. At length, on June 6, 1899, the prospectus of the proposed new company was published and the state of Whiteley's prosperity revealed in figures. The business was said to be carrying on thirty distinct branches of retail trading, and to have 113 different addresses in London. Its assets were valued at £1,601,216 in all, and the annual net profits for the preceding five years were returned as follows:

Year ending February 1895	£101,649
" " " 1896	£99,692
" " " 1897	£110,888
" " " 1898	£91,361
" " " 1899	£96,573

The business was to be capitalized at £1,800,100, half of which was to take the form of shares, the other half of debentures. The share capital of £900,100 was divided into 450,000 $4\frac{1}{2}$ per cent. cumulative preference shares of £1 each, 450,000 ordinary shares of £1 each, and 100 management shares of £1 each. The issue of management shares was a device imitated from Harrod's, such shares being reserved for the benefit of the directors or heads of departments in the firm, so enabling them to participate in any future growth of prosperity. But, contrary to expectation, none of this share capital was offered to the investing public. It was all taken by Whiteley himself as the price of handing over his business to the new company. The outside investor was offered merely the opportunity of buying 450,000 4 per cent. irredeemable first-mortgage debentures issued at £102 for every £100 worth of stock. The *Financial Times* tartly commented:

> In other words, Mr Whiteley is simply borrowing close upon a million of money at a little under 4 per cent. without giving the public any chance of participating in the profits of his business. We regard this not only as bad finance, but as extremely bad policy from the business point of view. Thousands upon thousands of Whiteley's customers have been looking forward to the forthcoming conversion of the business into a limited liability company in the hope that they might obtain an allotment of shares, and we have little doubt also that a large number of people have been induced to deal with the firm for the same reason. All these persons will be bitterly disappointed, and it would be hardly in human nature if a fair proportion of them did not show their disappointment by transferring their custom elsewhere.

The same paper pointed out that the figures of profits which had been disclosed seemed to indicate that the business was declining rather than expanding, as they included the Jubilee Year 1897, which was an exceptionally good one for shopkeepers. The figures included no allowance to Mr Whiteley for management, nor did they include the interest on moneys deposited with him. The assets had been valued entirely by Whiteley himself, and made insufficient allowance for depreciation of the leaseholds held by the firm. It was also noted that the statement of profits in the prospectus did not include the accounts of the working of the farms at Hillingdon and Hanworth, although the capital value of these estates was included among the assets.

In spite, however, of these and other critical comments, the general public eagerly subscribed for the debentures. Even before the prospectus had been issued they had been run up on the Stock Exchange to a premium of 9½ per cent.: that is, there were persons willing to buy at over £111 stock to be issued at £102. On the day of issue the rush to take up the debentures was so great that within a few hours the issue was subscribed more than seven times over. True, within a couple of months they had fallen back to £106; but even so they still stood at a premium over issue.

The taking over of the business by the new company seemed at first to signify but a nominal change in the responsibility for the concern. Whiteley still presided as chairman over the new board of directors, which included his two sons and his trusty manager, James Keith. The principal newcomer upon the scene was Samuel Wheeler, who had given up an important position as Official Receiver to the Board of Trade in favour of a seat on Whiteley's board as representative of the debenture shareholders. At the first annual dinner since the formation of the company—that is, on November 11, 1899—in the midst of many self-congratulatory speeches on the firm's prosperity and on the honour achieved by two young members of the staff who had been selected from the Kildare Ambulance Club for service in the field in the Boer War, a somewhat discordant note was struck by Samuel Wheeler, who hinted that there were already differences of opinion among the directors. The fact was that the debenture shareholders were none too pleased to find that Whiteley had included the value of his farms in the assets taken over by the company, as they were losing rather than making money. The differences between Wheeler and Whiteley on this issue were only eventually settled by the Universal Provider's offer to lease personally the farm properties from the company for an annual rent.

And so the twentieth century dawned over a business that in its enterprise, flamboyant self-confidence, and rapid rise to almost fabulous prosperity seemed to stand for the very essence of Victorian achievement. Its shops, farms, and factories now covered 250 acres of land. There were (1906) 159 departments, besides an estate agency, furniture factory and repository, dyeing and cleaning works, laundry, nurseries, and local delivery depots in five London suburbs. All these gave employment to 6000 hands. The business had a turnover of more than a million pounds a year, 10 per cent. of which represented net profit. Eleven to twelve thousand letters were delivered to Whiteley's every day, and required a staff of nearly fifty clerks to deal with them. Meanwhile the founder of it all, now a septuagenarian, but "hale, hearty, buoyant, rich in anecdote, a rare *raconteur,* in fact, and absolutely tireless," was beginning to withdraw himself a little from contact with the outer world. He was no longer interested in audacious pieces of publicity. Occasionally he would be sought out and his opinion be asked in a Press interview on some burning question of the day, such as

Protection, when he would give utterance to some characteristic boast, such as "I extended my business so as to provide all the world with what all the world requires, from its cradle to its bier. The world is my parish." And in 1902 T. P. O'Connor secured from him a chapter of autobiography describing his early life and struggles; this was published in *Mainly about People*. But for the most part Whiteley enveloped himself in that dignified silence which those who have lived their lives fully, and are satisfied with its results, prefer in their ripe old age. A quiet end, however, was not what fate had in store for the Universal Provider.

CHAPTER VII

Out of the Past

SHORTLY after midday on January 24, 1907, a young man entered Lancaster Gate Tube Station, on the Central London Railway, deposited a small parcel in the cloakroom, and, having left the station, walked rapidly in the direction of Westbourne Grove. He was about twenty-seven years of age, of medium height, slim in build, clean-shaven, and of fair complexion—altogether a handsome young man, except for an odd staring look in his eyes. He was well dressed in a frock-coat and silk hat, and was obviously well educated and a gentleman. At about half-past twelve he knocked at the door of No. 31 Porchester Terrace and inquired for Mr William Whiteley. The door was answered by the butler, who informed the visitor that Whiteley was out, being at his place of business in Westbourne Grove, less than a quarter of a mile from the house. Upon receiving this answer the young man went away, and a few minutes later entered the premises of the Universal Provider and repeated the request he had made at Porchester Terrace. As he did not give his name or business he was directed to a desk in No. 43 Westbourne Grove, where sat Daniel Goodman, the chief cashier, who asked whether he had an appointment. The young man replied " No," but added that he had come from Sir George Lewis, and that if Goodman would mention this fact to Mr Whiteley the latter would see him. Impressed by the name of this eminent lawyer, whose managing clerk he took the visitor to be (as a matter of fact, Sir George Lewis had on several occasions acted for Whiteley in the management of his private affairs), the cashier took the message in to Whiteley's private office, and returned with instructions to admit the young man. Goodman therefore carried out his instructions, and saw Whiteley greet his caller without any appearance of recognition, and wave him in his usual affable manner to a seat before closing the door of the office.

It was the concluding week of the January sale; the shops were thronged with customers, and business was active. Whiteley was at all times accessible to visitors, but it was his rule to allow no more than five minutes' interview to a casual caller. Moreover, he always lunched punctually at one o'clock, and used without fail to emerge from his room a few minutes before the hour for that purpose. It was therefore a matter of some surprise that this particular interview should have lasted nearly half an hour without interruption, except from a correspondence clerk who entered the room with some papers during its course, only to be told by Whiteley, "I can't see you now; I hope to see you presently." At four minutes past one, however, the door of the office was suddenly flung open, and the Universal Provider emerged from his room, evidently not in his usual state of affability and calm. He looked pale and agitated, and at once called out to one of his assistants to go out and fetch a policeman—presumably for the purpose of ridding himself of his visitor. Before this order could be carried out, however, the latter appeared behind Whiteley in the door of the office, and attempted to reopen a conversation that had evidently been going on between them. "Won't you come in again?" asked the young man. " No, no!" replied Whiteley. " Go away! If you don't I shall fetch a policeman."

" Aren't you going to come back?" asked the young man excitedly. " Is that your final word?"

" Yes."

" Then you are a dead man, Mr Whiteley"—and with those words the mysterious visitor drew a revolver from his left breast pocket, presented it close to Whiteley's head, and fired two shots. The first penetrated his victim's left cheek, the second entered his head behind the right ear and proved immediately fatal. The old man, now in his seventy-sixth year, reeled and fell to the ground, where life became extinct before anyone could reach him. Meanwhile his assailant forthwith placed his revolver to his own head and fired a third shot, which entered the left temple. He too tottered, and fell beside the man he had just killed. The shop where these scenes of violence took place was crowded with customers and assistants, but in spite of the appalling suddenness of the tragedy no time was lost in sending away the former, screening off the bodies, and summoning doctors and police. Dr French, of Porchester Gardens, and Dr Angus, surgeon of the local police division, arrived together and made a hasty examination of the two shot men. Whiteley, they found, had been killed instantaneously, but his assailant, though obviously seriously wounded, was still breathing, and even appeared to be conscious of his surroundings. He gave his name as Cecil Whiteley, and while he was being placed in an ambulance to be taken to St Mary's Hospital said, " I know what I have done. I am quite aware of what I have done." While Whiteley's body was being removed to the mortuary at Paddington Green all his

HORACE GEORGE RAYNER

From *The Illustrated London News*

shops in Westbourne Grove and Queen's Road were quickly closed, and a notice posted on the shutters: "Owing to the death of Mr Whiteley this establishment will be closed for the remainder of to-day (Thursday)." News of the murder was soon spread through the district and caused a painful sensation, not only throughout London, but as far away as Leeds and Wakefield, where Whiteley was well known. Whiteley's annual staff concert, which was to have been held that night in Queen's Hall, was naturally postponed.

The first thought of Detective-Inspector Fuller when he began to investigate the mystery was to search Whiteley's office for clues disclosing what might have taken place at the interview between Whiteley and his assailant. He therefore fetched Whiteley's solicitor, St John Roche, and together they went through the Universal Provider's papers, but found nothing which threw any light upon the tragedy. A message sent to Sir George Lewis brought back the reply that he had never sent anyone to see Whiteley, and was most distressed that his name should have been used by a stranger. The Inspector next possessed himself of the weapon used by the assailant, a six-chambered Colt revolver, fully loaded with soft-nosed or 'dum-dum' bullets, three of which had been fired. One of these bullets was afterwards found buried under some stock in the fur and lace department, close to where the murder took place. A search of the young man's person yielded one shilling in cash, several pawn-tickets relating to jewellery, a passport and other papers bearing the names of Thomas Smith, Payne, and Rayner. In the breast pocket of his coat were two small leaves, evidently torn from a pocket-book, which was subsequently traced by means of a receipt folded in the lining of his silk hat to the parcel he had deposited earlier that morning in Lancaster Gate cloakroom. On these two leaves were written in pencil this revealing message:

> To all whom it may concern: William Whiteley is my father, and has brought upon himself and me a double fatality by reason of his own refusal of a request perfectly reasonable. R.I.P.

This message suggested to the police that the assailant must have been trying to blackmail Whiteley, and had resorted to violence when the latter refused to be intimidated. In hospital the young man hovered between life and death, but during his lucid intervals he kept declaring that Whiteley was his father, and that he was "jolly glad" he had shot him because of the way in which he had treated his mother. On the day after the crime an operation was performed with the purpose of saving his life; three pieces of bullet were extracted from his head, and the right eye was removed. The bullet had also broken the bone at the base of his nose, but fortunately did not otherwise fracture the skull. To this event the miserable man owed his life. During subsequent weeks he was slowly and carefully nursed back to so-called health, in order that he might be brought to face the inevitable charge of murder.

Bit by bit the police pieced together the chain of events which had brought about the tragedy. The young man was that same Horace George Rayner who more than a dozen years previously had been told by Whiteley's former friend George Rayner that he was really a son of the Universal Provider. Since that time young Rayner had followed a strangely adventurous career. For a while he had worked in George

Rayner's office, but had parted from him at the age of seventeen after a quarrel, in order to take advantage of an offer to go abroad to Russia. Here he secured employment as overseer and cashier in the offices of a great meat firm, Vestey Brothers' Union Cold Storage Company, at Kosloff. But he lived a wild and extravagant life, and was said to have absconded eventually from his employers with £400 of the firm's money. Returning to London, he next changed his name to Horace Payne, and in 1899 took a post as correspondence clerk in the firm of Tubes, Ltd. His mother had just died at Southampton, one of her last messages to her son being that if he were ever in want of a friend he would find one in William Whiteley if he were to mention her name. With her death and last message still fresh in his mind Rayner found himself thrown a good deal into the society of his aunt Louisa, in whose company he met, for the first and only time, Cecil Whiteley and learned who he was. Perhaps this meeting confirmed him in his belief that he too was a son of the Universal Provider; at any rate, that Christmas he confided the notion to his chief—the first time, so far as is known, that he had spoken of it to an outsider. But he did not stay long in the employment of Tubes, Ltd., leaving after only two years to become private secretary to a diplomat, Sir Henry Burdett.

Imagining, perhaps, that a career was at length opening up before him, Rayner now took the step of marrying, on November 23, 1901, Alice May Knowles, the daughter of a Birmingham engineer. The couple had become acquainted at Bewdley, where Miss Knowles lived in a pretty villa by the Severn under the care of her two aunts, the Misses Knowles. The object of Rayner's visit to Bewdley was to meet the two children of his mother, Emily Turner, by George Rayner; but during his visit, in spite of being a Catholic, he attended the Anglican church, and there met Miss Knowles. Two children were born of this marriage, but Rayner never succeeded in making a sufficiently regular livelihood to provide his family with a permanent home. He was always in and out of jobs. Thus, after leaving Sir Henry Burdett, he attempted to enter the Consular Service, without success, and subsequently was employed by an hotel company for three years, until a change in the directorate led to his dismissal. He next began to borrow money from his wife's aunts, with the idea of setting up as a commission agent. This plan failing, he left his wife and two children to be looked after by the aunts, and betook himself in 1904 to Rhyl, in Wales, where he announced his intention of setting up in business as auctioneer and estate agent. He kept an office open here for about eighteen months, but entirely failed to build up a connexion, and in the autumn of 1905 suddenly left the country and returned to Russia. This visit, however, lasted only four months, and in March 1906 he was back again in London.

By this time the Misses Knowles had taken rooms for Mrs Rayner and her children in the house of a Mr Browning in Highgate, quarters which must have been miserable enough, seeing that the rent was only 5*s*. 6*d*. a week. Here Rayner joined his family and lived till September, when Browning removed to fresh quarters in Tottenham, taking with him his lodgers, whose rent now rose to seven shillings a week. The family remained here for the next three months, furnishing their rooms on the hire-purchase system, but being unable to maintain the payments, since Rayner, in spite of efforts to find employment, was always out of work and hard up and forced to resort to the pawnshops. At length the family had to leave their lodgings and disperse. Mrs Rayner and the children returned to Bewdley to the aunts, while Rayner himself, about the turn of the year, resorted to Rowton House, in Hammersmith, the recognized home of the 'down and outs.' On January 3, 1907, he took up his abode in a small private hotel at 23 Red Lion Street, run by one Jacob Gerhard, a place where he had stayed once before four years ago for a single night under the name of Horace Payne. This time, however, he registered under the name of Rayner. He occupied himself with further efforts to obtain employment and with the promotion of various fantastic schemes for making a livelihood. Thus he constantly inserted advertisements in newspapers, offering home employment of various kinds to women, such as colouring picture postcards. Meanwhile he maintained his credit with the hotel-keeper by boasting to him from time to time of his rich father—"a Yorkshireman, a millionaire, the richest man in London," as he described him, from whom he was shortly expecting a thousand pounds. Obviously whatever steadiness his character may ever have possessed was now deserting him. He was posing as a single man and apparently paying attentions to a barmaid, Dora Westwood, who was employed at the Horseshoe Hotel, Tottenham Court Road. And, in spite of the fact that he could now only keep himself alive by pawning his last possessions, he promised Dora to marry her, with a view to emigrating and making a fresh start. His irregular life, lack of employment, and deficiency of food had reduced him to a low state of health, in which his erratic tendencies became more and more pronounced. Again and again his thoughts reverted to the obsession that he was a son of the great William Whiteley. When he was at Rowton House at Christmas he had first thought of suicide, but at that moment his revolver had been in pawn. He now possessed himself again of his weapon, and turned over in his mind the question whether or not he would be justified in going to Westbourne Grove and interviewing the man whom he had not seen since his boyhood—over twenty years ago, in fact. By January 23 he had become so desperate that he resolved either to do something to help himself or to put an end to his privations by suicide. Accordingly, that afternoon he purchased from a gunsmith in the Strand a box of fifty 'police' cartridges, containing 'dum-dum' bullets, and later that evening instructed Gerhard to have him called early the following morning, as he had an appointment with a gentleman on money matters. On the 24th he rose at eight, left the hotel at half-past nine, and made his way, as has been already told, to Lancaster Gate tube station, where he left, in the name of H. D. Richards, a parcel of miscellaneous property, which included a passport, nineteen pawn-tickets, a notebook, and some advertisements. He had then in his pockets sixpence in coppers and a sixpenny bit.

This was the wretched story brought to light by the police investigations. It seemed to leave no doubt that Rayner had planned his crime in advance, and had

MRS WHITELEY AND MR FRANK WHITELEY LEAVING THE CORONER'S COURT AFTER THE INQUEST ON WILLIAM WHITELEY

From *The Illustrated London News*

gone to Whiteley with the intention of blackmailing him. Indeed, for some weeks after the Universal Provider's death sensational stories appeared in the Press to the effect that he had been for many years a victim of blackmailers, who had made the old man's life wretched and extracted large sums from him. But no facts whatever ultimately came to light in support of these stories. Instead, it became clear that Rayner and Whiteley had not set eyes upon each other since the former's boyhood, and that Rayner's crime must therefore be an isolated act performed without accomplices. On January 28, at the inquest held at the Paddington Coroner's Court, the jury returned a verdict of "Wilful murder" against Rayner, who was thereupon handed over to the police. Public curiosity had been greatly roused by the mysterious nature of the case, and speculations were freely expressed as to whether Rayner might or might not really be a son of Whiteley. As Emily Turner was dead few persons were in a position to throw much light on the problem; but one of these was George Rayner, who, after the inquest, directed his solicitors to issue a Press statement on his behalf. In this statement George Rayner made it clear that he repudiated the paternity of Horace George Rayner. He declared that Emily Turner had improperly registered her son under this name, and that the only name the latter was entitled to was that of Turner. George Rayner admitted, indeed, that he had made a promise to Emily Turner that he would act as foster-father to the boy Horace—a promise which he had carried out, but which must not be taken to imply that he acknowledged him as his son. This statement on behalf of Rayner obviously did nothing to clear up the mystery, and left the question of Horace George Rayner's paternity as uncertain as before.

It was not till February 19 that the ill-fated young man whose name was thus in doubt was sufficiently restored to health to be able to appear in court. That morning he was discharged from hospital and taken into custody by the police, and later in the same day he was formally charged before the magistrate at Marylebone with the murder of Whiteley. He was then in such a feeble state of health that he had to be conveyed to prison in a cab. On February 26 and again on March 5 he made further appearances in the police-court, where his previous history was recounted by the prosecution, and sufficient evidence was given to cause the magistrate to commit him for trial at the Central Criminal Court. So at length, on Friday, March 22, the last act of the drama was played out, and Rayner took his stand in the dock at the new Old Bailey, in a court presided over by Lord Alverstone, the Lord Chief Justice of England. Mr R. D. Muir and Mr Arthur Gill appeared for the Director of Public Prosecutions; Mr George Elliott and Mr Henry Curtis Bennett (afterwards Sir Henry Curtis Bennett) were retained for the defence; Mr Bodkin appeared for the Whiteley family; and Mr Lloyd held a watching brief for George Rayner. Although Rayner pleaded "Not guilty" to the charge of murdering Whiteley, the real issue in the case was not his guilt, but his state of mind. For many weeks previously public opinion had been greatly stirred by the course of an American murder trial which in some of its features resembled the Whiteley affair. Only

From *The Penny Illustrated Paper*, March 30, 1907

in this case it was a millionaire, Thaw, who had committed a particularly brutal murder in a fit of passion, and his vast wealth was being employed by his relatives to enable him to escape the supreme penalty by proving him to have been temporarily insane at the time when he committed the crime. The proceedings had been protracted in scandalous fashion week after week, alienists and specialists being called to give expert evidence for and against Thaw's madness. Eventually the weight of wealth told, and Thaw escaped the electric chair. Meanwhile in England it was the poor man who had murdered the millionaire; and the more intelligent and humane sections of public opinion were wondering whether or not Rayner would be treated with the full rigour of the law. Was there any loophole in English law which might enable him to plead temporary insanity with the slightest chance of success? Orthodox opinion, of course, scouted the idea, *The Times* voicing this point of view in an article which contrasted favourably the consistency and rigidity of English justice with the venality and sentimentality of American justice. But any idea that Rayner could successfully plead insanity was soon dispelled by the course of the trial, since even the two doctors who were called for the defence (Dr Shaw and Dr Mercier) could not say more than that the prisoner had suffered from mental instability and diminished self-control, which might account for his committing an act from which he would recover without knowing what had happened. They explained that his ancestry, his drinking habits, his want of regular food, and his distress of mind from poverty and worry would certainly render him more susceptible to a sudden impulse at a moment of crisis. But they agreed that he was not insane in a legal or medical sense.

The central features of the trial were not, therefore, Rayner's guilt or innocence, or even his sanity or insanity, but the possibility that light might be thrown upon the two hitherto unexplained mysteries of the case—Rayner's paternity and the details of what passed at the interview between him and Whiteley. There were but two persons remaining alive who could throw any clear light on these questions. Louisa Turner alone perhaps knew the secret of her sister, Emily; and Rayner himself alone knew what Whiteley and he had said to each other during that last half-hour in the counting-house in Westbourne Grove. George Rayner, it is true, was also alive, but he was not put into the witness-box—perhaps because it was realized that he had nothing more to say than was contained in the statement he had already issued through his solicitors. Louisa Turner, however, was available, and was called by the prosecution to give evidence. Intense curiosity was roused among those in court when she entered the box. Fifty-one years old, and wearing eyeglasses, but still slim and graceful, she indicated by her appearance the attractions she must have possessed in her youth. Yet Louisa Turner had no revelations to make that had not already been suggested in some quarter or another before the trial began. If she knew the real secret of Horace George Rayner's birth she did not reveal it. Step by step she was taken by the lawyers over the ground of the story, now twenty-five to thirty years old, of the tangled relations between Whiteley, George Rayner, and the two Turner sisters. She gave no indication of the possibility of any intimate connexion between Whiteley and Emily, although in giving details of the *ménage* in Greville Road, Kilburn, she revealed several curious and somewhat inconsistent facts with regard to Whiteley's use of Rayner's name when it suited him. Clearly the relations between the two men and the two sisters must have been at times sufficiently tangled to account for the possibility of their misinterpretation by a curious child. But Louisa's evidence was on the whole consonant with her natural sense of loyalty towards Whiteley. At the point where she was questioned about the final quarrel between George Rayner and Whiteley over herself she indicated that the allegations made by the latter about herself and Rayner were without foundation. And when she left the witness-box the mystery of Horace George's birth remained as dark as it had always been.

While the prosecution through the mouth of Mr Muir stressed the " great care and deliberation " with which Rayner had planned his crime, Mr George Elliott for the defence declared that it was no part of his case to prove or allege that the prisoner was, in fact, a son of Whiteley, but only that he had rightly or wrongly believed he was Whiteley's son, and that this belief preyed upon his mind and, when he was sunk in poverty, came home to him as a fact so vital to his life's future that it determined his actions. Describing Rayner's pitiful and unsuccessful attempts to make a career, found a family, and earn a livelihood, Mr Elliott pointed out that " all this operated gradually upon a mind never of a powerful equilibrium and on a body enfeebled by the drinking tendencies of his mother, grandmother, and great-grandmother."

He was not, indeed, legally insane, but he was a degenerate, whose mental heritage was tainted by at least two generations of alcohol. In many matters he was shrewd, clever, and accomplished, but he suffered from mental explosions, and at certain moments was guilty of acts of "impulsive insanity." Mr Elliott argued that Rayner had premeditated his own suicide, but not the murder of Whiteley, and that he had committed the actual crime in a moment of "black-out," when he did not know what he was doing.

Among the most pathetic figures in court were Mrs Rayner, who was shortly to bear her third child, and the two Misses Knowles, who in turn gave evidence both as to the prisoner's poverty and privations, and as to his strange manner, fits of depression, sleepless nights, and "a hunted kind of look." None of them had been aware of Rayner's assumed connexion with Whiteley, though the aunts remembered him saying that he had a great secret in his life which weighed down his mind. After this the prisoner himself went into the box. Having been taken by Mr Elliott point by point through the history of his life, with its misty recollections of contacts with Whiteley in boyhood, he came at length to what transpired during the fatal interview on January 24, 1907.

> MR ELLIOTT: "Will you tell us what led up to your going to see Mr Whiteley?"
>
> RAYNER (speaking deliberately): "Well, I think, and still consider, that I had ample grounds for calling on Mr Whiteley for assistance—at least of the kind for which I asked."

Rayner then proceeded to describe his interview with Whiteley:

" We sat facing each other. He said, 'What can I do for you?' I said, 'I believe I am right in stating that a son is speaking to his father?' He said, 'Is that so? And when did you see me last?' I mentioned a circumstance that I used to live at Greville Road. I said I had seen him there. Mr Whiteley said, 'What can I do for you?' I mentioned the desperate straits I was in, my wife's condition. I made no proposition as to monetary help from him at the time. After further conversation, and as I was not getting much nearer to the object of my visit, I put it to him, 'Can you assist me in any way?' Mr Whiteley said, 'I cannot recall the past,' or words to that effect. He also said, 'It is all very fine, but there are two sides to every question,' and that I had only heard one side. Mr Whiteley then asked if I would like to go abroad. I said that needed capital. He said, 'Many young fellows go abroad and do well without having started with capital. I should advise you to go to the Salvation Army.' I was very much nettled at this, seeing so little sentiment, and I had a considerable revulsion of feeling in my mind. I said, 'Do you absolutely refuse to help me, either in kind or in employment?' He said, 'Yes.' 'Then,' I said, 'I must tell you I have made up my mind to blow my brains out if I am unsuccessful.' Mr Whiteley said, 'Don't talk so silly!' I produced a revolver and put it to my head. He said, 'Put that thing down!' And I put it behind my back. My head was in a whirl. I still had a feeling of revulsion in my mind that he should have treated me so badly, and I thought, if he is not amenable to sentiment and sense of duty, he may be amenable to a sense of fear; and I made up my mind to play that last card, with no intention of carrying it into effect.

" So I put the revolver back in my pocket and tore two leaves out of a pocket-book and started to write. Mr Whiteley sat opposite me. He got up and went to the door. I said, 'Won't you wait?' But he took no notice. My head was in a state of blankness, and I did not know what to do, having practically condemned myself to death. I got up and opened the door to see what had become of Mr

Whiteley. I went towards him and extended my hand in a friendly way. I asked him to come in again, and he said to me, 'No. I will say no more.' I said, 'Is that your final word?' or something of that kind. He said, 'Yes. I have sent for a policeman.' This is all I remember of the circumstances. The actual shots and what was in my mind I do not remember. The last I remember is his statement that he had sent for a policeman."

Needless to say, the prisoner's statement created a sensation in the crowded court. It had a ring of truth about it, and if accepted seemed to show that Whiteley had certainly not manifested his well-known tact and philanthropy during the interview with his strange caller. That the truth of Rayner's statement was accepted by the court was shown by the fact that Mr Muir waived all cross-examination of the prisoner—an occurrence which must surely be almost without parallel in murder trials where the prisoner has pleaded "Not guilty" and subsequently gone into the witness-box. It was, indeed, possible, in the light of Rayner's history and this statement, mentally to reconstruct the whole sequence of events in such a way as to make it appear credible that he had hardly known what he was doing when he fired the fatal shots. But the plea of "impulsive insanity" suffered from one fatal flaw—the letter scrawled by Rayner on the two leaves torn from his pocket-book, in which he spoke of a "double fatality" being brought down upon his own and Whiteley's head.

After Mr Muir had submitted for the prosecution that there was no evidence to go to the jury that the prisoner was insane, and the Lord Chief Justice had accepted his contention, the summing up and verdict which followed were inevitable. Lord Alverstone emphasized the fact that the test of insanity—whether or not a man was in a mental condition to be responsible for his actions—was whether the jury were satisfied that at the time the act was committed the accused did not know the distinction between right and wrong, or else was not in a condition to appreciate the quality of his act. The mere fact that a man had a rooted belief which might or might not have a foundation was no indication at all that he was insane according to the legal definition of insanity. In fine, the Lord Chief Justice told the jury to dismiss from their minds any question whether the prisoner was insane or not insane when the act was done, because both his previous life and his conduct at the time left no loophole or grounds for supposing that he did not know perfectly well what he was doing.

At the conclusion of the summing up the jury retired only for ten minutes before returning with a verdict of "Guilty." In answer to the usual question Rayner, who had remained perfectly composed throughout the trial, declared he had nothing to say; whereupon the Lord Chief Justice sentenced him to death in the usual way, adding this brief observation:

> "Horace George Rayner, I will not harrow the feelings of those who hear me or of yourself by any reference to this terrible crime of which you have been convicted on the most conclusive evidence—a crime which showed deliberation and determination to revenge yourself upon a man if you could not succeed in obtaining from him the assistance you hoped he would give you. I cannot hold out to you the slightest hope that the sentence of the law will not be carried into effect, and I call upon you most earnestly to spend the time which may be allowed to you in earnest communion with your Maker."

From the legal point of view Rayner's fate was now sealed—indeed, the Lord Chief Justice seemed to have gone out of his way to dispel any hope of a reprieve. But the whole course of the trial, and more particularly the fact that Rayner had been carefully nursed back from death's door in order to face his ordeal, had profoundly influenced public opinion in his favour. On March 26 *The Times* published a letter from Rayner's solicitor, H. Pierron, stating that he was preparing a petition to the Home Secretary for a commutation of the sentence, and inviting public support. Within two days no fewer than 4000 letters applying for petition forms for the collection of signatures had been received from all parts of the world, many containing gifts of money for Mrs Rayner. A committee of ladies was set up to carry on the work, and a surprising proportion of signatures to the petition came in from clergymen, politicians, people of title, and, oddly enough, according to *The Times*, "employees of Metropolitan Borough Councils." A separate petition was received from the employees of the Carriage and Wagon Depot of the Midland Railway, and a member of the jury which had found Rayner guilty worked actively to secure his reprieve. Among the strange collection of letters received by Pierron was one from an unknown female who offered to substitute herself for Rayner on the scaffold, and invited a reply through the 'agony' columns of a morning newspaper. At the City Temple the Reverend R. J. Campbell, in the course of a service, announced that he had thought the matter over carefully, and had come to the conclusion that he would ask his audience to sign the petition if they could do so conscientiously. His remark that "the heart of England has been touched with pity for this young man" was received with cheers from the congregation, many of whom subsequently signed the petition.

Within little more than a week from the trial 180,000 signatures to the petition had been obtained, and it was confidently believed that by April 1, when Pierron proposed to present it to the Home Secretary, the number would amount to half a million. But behind the scenes the Home Office was acting with unusual promptitude. In reply to a question in Parliament asked by Mr John Ward on March 27 the Home Secretary, Mr Gladstone, promised to take into consideration the unusual and peculiar circumstances of Rayner's case; and on the 31st he wrote to Pierron saying that "in view of all the circumstances he had felt warranted in advising his Majesty to respite the capital sentence with a view to commutation to penal servitude for life." The news was received with joy by Mrs Rayner, but when the prisoner, who was in Pentonville, had the information conveyed to him all he could say was that "so far as he personally was concerned, he would have preferred to get the whole business over and done with, instead of having to endure years of misery behind iron bars." And in this understandable attitude he persisted, for on October 21, 1907, he attempted to commit suicide in his cell bed at Parkhurst Prison by opening an artery in his wrist, and in April 1908 he was charged before the visiting magistrate with having set fire to his prison bedding. The result of these two outbursts was to bring upon himself periods of solitary confinement with bread-and-water diet. Yet Rayner's sufferings

PAGE FROM "THE PENNY ILLUSTRATED PAPER" AT THE TIME OF THE AGITATION FOR RAYNER'S REPRIEVE

must have inclined authority to take a lenient view of his offences. Reprieved murderers are almost invariably called upon to serve a sentence of at least twenty years' imprisonment, but Rayner was released from prison in 1919, after only twelve years' incarceration.

Meanwhile the victim of his crime had been borne with every circumstance of honour to his last resting-place. Whiteley's funeral took place on January 30, 1907. All his own shops (except the bank) were closed that day to enable the staff to attend the ceremony. Most shops in the neighbourhood, too, put up large perpendicular black boards on their windows, lowered their flags to half-mast, and closed their doors for the morning. The funeral *cortège* started from Whiteley's mansion, 31 Porchester Terrace, at half-past eleven, but for the previous half-hour the street had become impassable for ordinary traffic by reason of the dense crowds that thronged it, requiring a police cordon to keep them in check. First came five open carriages, all filled with flowers (over two hundred wreaths were received); next the coffin of the Universal Provider in an open hearse, also covered with flowers; and, lastly, nearly a hundred carriages, two-thirds of which carried Whiteley's staff, the remainder members of the family and friends. The coffin bore a plain brass plate inscribed simply, "William Whiteley, aged 75 years. Died January 24th, 1907." Prominent upon it lay a floral harp with a broken string, sent by Mrs Whiteley, "In saddest memory." Slowly the *cortège* wound its way from Porchester Terrace to Christ Church, Lancaster Gate, for the first part of the burial service. The house-tops all along the route and the flats of projecting shops were full of spectators, while a great crowd marched silently behind in procession. After the service the *cortège* proceeded back to Kensal Green Cemetery, where the coffin was lowered into the family grave, and all was over. At the graveside stood, among Whiteley's other friends and relatives, Sir Thomas Lipton and representatives of the main organizations in the shopping trade.

After the funeral the family gathered at the house in Porchester Terrace to hear the family solicitor, St John Roche, read the will. There was, as became known later when the estate had been proved, £1,452,825 gross to dispose of. The Universal Provider had never during his lifetime distinguished himself by large gifts to charities, though he had often displayed generosity on special occasions to individuals and organizations. But now his will revealed that he had been saving up his charities for a single mighty bequest which would provide a permanent memorial of him after his death. The will, dated 1904, left legacies ranging from £2000 to £100 to various hospitals, an annuity of £1000 to each of his daughters, and £50,000 to be held in trust for each of his sons. Mrs Whiteley was left nothing beyond the life provision already made for her under the separation deed. Then came two further substantial legacies—£5000 for "Whiteley Christmas Gifts" to be distributed to the poor of Paddington, and £5000 to the "Whiteley Sports Trustees" to provide prizes for the encouragement of cricket, football, rowing, and swimming among persons residing within a radius of five miles from Westbourne Grove. Lastly, a sum as near as possible to a million pounds was to be paid over to the "Whiteley Homes Trustees" in order to found, provide, and maintain "Whiteley Homes for the Aged Poor," and to help maintain the inmates of these houses, who were to be men over sixty-five and women over sixty years of age. Ever since the Queen's Jubilee of 1887 Whiteley had taken an interest in the welfare of the aged poor, and this magnificent bequest was his way of showing how near to his heart stood the problem which only a year or two after his death was to be met by the State through the provision of old-age pensions. Whiteley left elaborate directions for the carrying out of his bequest; the trustees soon set to work, and the result can be seen to-day in the Whiteley Village, which stands on the western slopes of the valley of the river Mole, at Burhill, in Surrey.

But the business which had been the work of his life remains as a greater monument to his fame than the charity which he founded by his death. True, some of the glories of Victorian days have departed from Westbourne Grove. True, only a portion of the row of shops he established there is now occupied by the firm that bears his name. But the flag of William Whiteley, Ltd., still waves proudly in Queen's Road over the site of what was once the Paddington Baths—now a domed hall in a building loftier and more spacious than any of those which the founder erected. And under the ægis of Selfridge's Whiteley's to-day carries on the tradition handed down to it, a tradition summed up in the trademark coined seventy years ago with such self-confident, almost sacrilegious, daring by the man who might justly be called London's greatest shopkeeper—the "Universal Provider."

BIBLIOGRAPHY

ANSTEY, F.: *The Man from Blankley's* (1893).

BARNARD, ALFRED: *Orchards and Gardens* (1895).

BENNETT, A. R.: *London and Londoners in the Eighteen-fifties* (1924).

BRABAZON, LORD: *The Early Closing Movement* (1882).

—— *The Cause of the Overworked Shop Assistant* (1883).

Catalogue of the Great Exhibition of 1851.

FRITH, W. P.: *Autobiography and Reminiscences* (1887–88).

Handy Book of Shopkeeping, The (1866).

HUGHES, M. V.: *A London House in the Nineties* (1937).

JEVONS, W. S.: *State in Relation to Labour* (1882).

Linen Drapers' Magna Charta, The (1839).

MAXWELL, W. B.: *Reminiscences* (1938).

Reminiscences of an Old Draper (1876).

Report of the Lancet Sanitary Commission (1886).

Report of the Select Committee on Shop Hours (1886).

SUTHERST, T.: *Death and Disease Behind the Counter* (1884).

WARREN, S.: *Ten Thousand a Year* (1841).

WEY, F.: *A Frenchman Sees the English in the Fifties* (1935).

William Whiteley's Illustrated Catalogue and General Price List (1885).

PERIODICALS

The Bayswater Chronicle; *The Daily Chronicle*; *The Daily Graphic* (New York); *The Daily Telegraph*; *The Draper's Record*; *The Essex Weekly News*; *The Financial Times*; *The Kensington Express*; *The Lancet*; *Mainly About People*; *The News of the World*; *The Paddington Times*; *The Pall Mall Gazette*; *Punch*; *The Times*; *Truth*; *Whiteley's Diary and Almanac.*

INDEX

Index

S

Index

Index

Lightning Source UK Ltd.
Milton Keynes UK
UKHW011954191021
392485UK00002B/504

9 781406 724288